AURORA

THE HYPERLOOP REVOLUTION

The New Era of Land Travel

2025

The Hyperloop Revolution

Aurora Amoris

CONTENTS

CHAPTER 1

Hyperloop: The Future of
Transportation

1.1. Definition of Hyperloop Technology

Hyperloop generation refers to a high-speed floor transportation machine that uses a low-stress tube to move pressurized pods at extraordinarily high velocities. These pods, additionally known as capsules, journey internal near-vacuum tubes, extensively lowering air resistance and friction, thereby enabling extraordinary speeds for land-based totally travel. The machine is designed to be incredibly green, the usage of magnetic levitation (maglev) or air bearings to allow pods to flow silently and with minimum strength consumption.

At its core, the Hyperloop idea merges a couple of superior technologies. A regular Hyperloop system accommodates a sealed tube or network of tubes thru which a pod may additionally journey free of air resistance or friction. The pod is both levitated the use of magnetic fields (electromagnetic or electrodynamic suspension) or thru an air cushion created by way of onboard compressors. Propulsion is achieved the usage of linear electric powered cars that boost up the pod through successive ranges along the tube's period.

The concept of the Hyperloop was popularized in 2013 by using Elon Musk through a white paper launched by means of SpaceX, even though the idea draws idea from in advance improvements in vacuum and pneumatic educate systems relationship again to the 19th century. What distinguishes the cutting-edge Hyperloop from previous attempts is the combination of modern-day technologies—including renewable energy assets, AI-driven control systems, superior substances, and self sufficient operation—to create a scalable, green, and sustainable shipping community.

By minimizing touch between vehicle and song, Hyperloop systems aim to reach speeds over 1,000 kilometers consistent with hour (620 mph), probably slicing travel instances between main towns from hours to mere minutes. Because the tubes are enclosed, the machine is likewise covered from climate conditions and outside environmental disruptions, providing a stage of reliability not often achievable with traditional transportation.

Hyperloop era isn't always just an development in pace but additionally in sustainability and protection. By the usage of electric propulsion and potentially relying entirely on renewable energy, it offers an environmentally friendly opportunity to fossil-gas-primarily based transportation systems. Moreover, its enclosed infrastructure is designed to limit the threat of injuries because of human mistakes, natural world, or climate.

Hyperloop technology represents a transformative bounce in transportation, combining vacuum tubes, maglev or air-bearing suspension, and electric propulsion to deliver ultrafast, green, and eco-friendly transit. Though nevertheless in the experimental and developmental levels, it has captured the hobby of governments, personal corporations, and researchers around the world, with severa tasks underway to carry this futuristic imaginative and prescient into reality.

1.2. The First Ideas and Initial Developments

The origins of Hyperloop technology may be traced again to conceptual transportation ideas that date as far again because the 19th century. The foundational idea — propelling a pill or pod thru a low-stress tube to reduce air resistance — turned into first hinted at in early pneumatic tube systems used in postal offerings. In the 1800s, inventors like George Medhurst anticipated atmospheric railways, the usage of air strain to push cars thru sealed tubes. Though rudimentary and restricted through the technology of the time, those early tries laid the foundation for the excessive-pace concepts that could follow.

A greater direct predecessor to Hyperloop appeared inside the 20th century. In the 1970s, researchers and engineers proposed ideas just like the "vactrain" — brief for vacuum train — which estimated passenger pods traveling via evacuated tubes at near-sonic speeds. Robert M. Salter of RAND Corporation wrote significantly on the idea, exploring its feasibility for military and civilian programs. The primary undertaking on the time remained technological boundaries, particularly in accomplishing and keeping vacuum conditions over lengthy distances and dealing with propulsion and braking systems efficiently.

The turning factor for Hyperloop came in 2013 when Elon Musk, CEO of Tesla and SpaceX, launched a white paper titled "Hyperloop Alpha." In this paper, Musk proposed a 5th mode of transportation — after automobiles, planes, boats, and trains — that might be faster, more secure, and more strength-efficient. His thought combined magnetic levitation (maglev) with low-stress tubes to allow pods to travel at speeds exceeding 700 miles consistent with hour. Unlike preceding vactrain proposals, Musk's concept emphasised electricity performance, value-effectiveness, and practicality in cutting-edge urban environments.

Musk's open-supply method in sharing the Hyperloop Alpha white paper ignited a worldwide interest amongst engineers, researchers, and marketers. Numerous startups emerged to take at the project of turning the concept into reality. Companies together with Virgin Hyperloop (previously Hyperloop One), Hardt Hyperloop, TransPod, and Zeleros commenced developing complete-scale prototypes and check tracks to validate the generation. These projects converted Hyperloop from a futuristic principle into a aggressive area of innovation and experimentation.

In parallel, academic establishments and scholar groups contributed to the momentum. The SpaceX Hyperloop Pod Competition, first launched in 2015, invited college groups to design and build prototype pods, fostering a new technology of engineers and sparking further traits. These competitions no longer handiest tested the feasibility of the core generation however also caused vital improvements in propulsion, protection, braking structures, and levitation mechanisms.

The first ideas and preliminary tendencies of Hyperloop era are rooted in centuries-old transportation theories, reimagined via 21st-century engineering and innovation. The fusion of vacuum tube principles with present day magnetic levitation and propulsion systems has transformed a as soon as-fantastical idea right into a tangible aim this is progressively moving from theoretical blueprints to actual-world packages.

1.3. Research and Development Process for Hyperloop

The research and development process of Hyperloop technology is an intricate journey shaped by visionary concepts, engineering challenges, and multidisciplinary collaborations. What began as a theoretical proposition has now evolved into a globally competitive technological race. This process can be best understood by tracing the key phases of advancement, from initial feasibility studies to full-scale prototypes and regulatory preparations.

The origins of Hyperloop's research and development are often linked to Elon Musk's 2013 white paper, which outlined a high-speed transportation system based on low-pressure tubes and magnetic levitation. While Musk himself encouraged others to develop the concept, companies like Virgin Hyperloop, Hyperloop Transportation Technologies (HTT), Hardt Hyperloop, and TransPod took up the challenge. These companies set up laboratories and test tracks, attracting global talent from fields including aerospace engineering, vacuum systems, materials science, and artificial intelligence.

One of the early priorities in the R&D process was the development of the tube infrastructure. Engineers needed to assess materials that could withstand atmospheric pressure differences, thermal expansion, and external environmental stresses. This led to the exploration of steel alloys, carbon fiber composites, and other materials that would balance strength, durability, and cost. Additionally, tube designs had to account for seismic activity, terrain variations, and environmental impact—prompting geotechnical studies and civil engineering innovations.

Parallel to infrastructure design, a significant part of the R&D process has focused on the propulsion system. Linear induction motors and magnetic levitation (maglev) technologies were adapted and modified to fit within the tube environment. The challenge was not only to achieve high-speed propulsion but to ensure precise control, safety, and minimal energy waste. This required the development of sophisticated control algorithms, redundant safety systems, and innovations in electromagnetic field containment.

Vacuum technology represented another frontier. The Hyperloop concept requires maintaining a near-vacuum state within the tube to minimize air resistance. Researchers and engineers developed vacuum pumps capable of sustaining ultra-low pressure across long distances. This involved collaboration with manufacturers of industrial vacuum equipment and the implementation of real-time monitoring systems to detect pressure fluctuations or leaks.

Passenger safety and comfort were also central to development efforts. Research into human tolerance to acceleration, deceleration, and environmental conditions inside the pods led to the design of ergonomic seats, vibration damping systems, and life support systems. Prototypes were tested with crash simulations, airlock trials, and emergency scenarios to ensure robustness under all possible conditions.

The R&D process further extended into digital domains. Artificial intelligence and machine learning models were employed to optimize route planning, energy consumption, and predictive maintenance. Digital twins—virtual replicas of Hyperloop systems—allowed engineers to simulate and refine operations before physical implementation, saving time and reducing risks.

Testing facilities played a crucial role in the R&D process. Companies established various test tracks such as DevLoop in Nevada and facilities in the Netherlands, Canada, and India.

These test sites allowed real-world trials of pod acceleration, levitation, braking, and docking systems. Each successful test informed the next iteration of design, contributing to a continuous cycle of improvement.

Collaboration with universities and research institutions became a strategic asset. Academic partnerships enabled access to high-end labs and provided an environment for theoretical modeling and peer-reviewed validation. Competitions like the SpaceX Hyperloop Pod Competition encouraged student-led innovation, bringing fresh ideas and accelerating progress.

Regulatory development has run in parallel with technical R&D. Since Hyperloop represents a new transportation category, companies have worked closely with government agencies to shape safety protocols, environmental assessments, and legal frameworks. Regulatory sandboxes have been established in some regions, allowing experimental operation under monitored conditions while full standards are being developed.

Funding is an ever-present factor in the R&D process. The high capital demands of Hyperloop projects necessitate a combination of venture capital, government grants, and public-private partnerships. Financial planning is critical to maintain momentum and avoid stagnation between testing phases.

Today, the research and development of Hyperloop technology stands at a pivotal point. While no full-scale passenger system is operational yet, the progress in testing, engineering design, and international collaboration suggests that Hyperloop may transition from concept to reality within the next decade. The R&D process has not only advanced technology but also reshaped how the world envisions the future of transportation—blending science, sustainability, and systemic innovation into a single transformative idea.

1.4. Key Features of Hyperloop Technology

The Hyperloop era stands as a groundbreaking innovation that redefines the future of transportation by means of combining velocity, performance, and sustainability in an unparalleled way. At its middle, Hyperloop operates with the aid of transporting passenger or shipment pods through near-vacuum tubes, extensively decreasing air resistance and taking into account remarkably high speeds with minimum strength intake. This fundamental characteristic distinguishes Hyperloop from any conventional mode of land journey.

One of the most defining factors of Hyperloop is its vacuum tube machine. By growing an environment where the air pressure inside the tube is significantly lowered—often by means of up to 99%—the pods face minimum aerodynamic drag. This reduction in resistance not best permits pods to accelerate to speeds surpassing 1,000 kilometers according to hour however additionally drastically decreases the strength required to maintain such speeds. Unlike conventional trains or motors that war atmospheric friction and turbulence, Hyperloop pills float nearly effects, promising smoother, quieter rides for passengers.

Another important function lies within the electromagnetic propulsion and levitation systems that strength Hyperloop pods. Instead of counting on wheels or conventional rails, Hyperloop uses magnetic levitation technology that permit the drugs to glide simply above the song surface. This close to-frictionless suspension ensures minimal mechanical wear and complements energy performance. Propulsion is executed through linear cars that generate electromagnetic fields, accelerating the pods easily and correctly along the tube. This mixture of magnetic levitation and propulsion not best will increase velocity however also appreciably improves ride consolation with the aid of getting rid of vibrations and bumps related to conventional rail travel.

Speed and energy performance are inextricably connected in the Hyperloop design. While airplanes and high-speed trains have set benchmarks for rapid tour, Hyperloop objectives to surpass those by way of presenting comparable or more speeds with far decrease energy consumption. The integration of vacuum tubes and electromagnetic propulsion approach electricity losses are minimized, and while mixed with renewable electricity sources like sun or wind strength, the device can perform with a dramatically reduced carbon footprint. This positions Hyperloop no longer just as a transportation breakthrough but as a version for environmentally sustainable mobility.

The gadget's modular and flexible layout further complements its adaptability and scalability. Hyperloop routes can be constructed in segments, taking into account incremental expansion and customization based on regional wishes. This modularity simplifies maintenance and upgrades, allowing sections of the tune or pods to be serviced independently with out disrupting the entire community. Such flexibility makes Hyperloop possible for numerous geographies and population densities, from densely packed city corridors to sprawling intercity connections.

Safety remains paramount in Hyperloop improvement. Pods are built using advanced, excessive-energy substances designed to face up to high-speed travel stresses and capability emergencies. The gadget employs comprehensive tracking technology to constantly investigate tube strain, pod integrity, and environmental conditions, enabling real-time responses to any anomalies. Automated protection protocols ensure pods can decelerate unexpectedly and accurately if needed, while redundant systems and fail-safes minimize dangers. This attention on safety extends to passenger comfort, with the layout emphasizing stability, noise reduction, and weather manipulate inside the drugs.

Hyperloop's ability to substantially lessen tour instances without sacrificing comfort marks some other progressive attribute. Journeys that historically take hours through car or conventional educate can be shortened to mere mins, opening new opportunities for commuting, commercial enterprise journey, and tourism. The clean ride, loose from bumps and noise pollutants standard of different transport modes, promises a travel revel in this is each speedy and enjoyable.

Furthermore, regenerative power systems are integrated into the Hyperloop design to recapture power throughout braking stages, feeding it again into the device and enhancing universal performance. This non-stop cycle of power restoration facilitates lessen working fees and supports the purpose of sustainable, low-effect transportation.

Finally, Hyperloop's infrastructure is designed to decrease its bodily footprint. Elevated tracks and narrow assist pillars lessen land usage, retaining herbal habitats and present urban landscapes. This thoughtful integration permits Hyperloop networks to weave via or above populated areas with minimum disruption, facilitating higher urban and nearby connectivity without significant environmental or social fees.

Hyperloop era combines an innovative vacuum tube environment, electromagnetic propulsion and levitation, unmatched speed, strength performance, modularity, superior safety measures, and a sustainable infrastructure design. These interwoven functions set up Hyperloop not most effective because the destiny of land journey however additionally as a transformative bounce in the direction of greener, faster, and more connected transportation worldwide.

1.5. Advantages Over Traditional Transportation

Hyperloop technology gives a paradigm shift in land transportation, offering a multitude of advantages over conventional modes including automobiles, trains, and airplanes. At the leading edge of those benefits is its unparalleled velocity. Unlike traditional rail or avenue shipping, Hyperloop tablets can attain velocities exceeding 1,000 kilometers per hour, drastically lowering journey instances among towns and regions. This ability to cover long distances in mere mins opens up new possibilities for commuting, commercial enterprise, and tourism, successfully shrinking geographical limitations and fostering extra economic integration.

In addition to hurry, Hyperloop's energy performance sticks out as a substantial advantage. Traditional transportation systems regularly depend on fossil fuels or consume huge quantities of electricity with tremendously low efficiency. In assessment, Hyperloop's aggregate of a close to-vacuum tube environment and electromagnetic propulsion minimizes friction and air resistance, allowing pods to journey at excessive speeds using notably much less power. When paired with renewable energy assets inclusive of solar panels established alongside the song or wind energy, Hyperloop systems can function with a notably smaller carbon footprint, making them a ways more sustainable than most current shipping options.

Safety is any other critical location where Hyperloop holds an area. Traditional vehicles and trains are challenge to numerous risks together with collisions, derailments, and weather-related disruptions. Hyperloop drugs, enclosed inside sealed tubes, are in large part isolated from outside environmental factors inclusive of climate or obstacles, lowering the hazard of injuries. Additionally, the system carries advanced automated controls, regular tracking, and emergency protocols that enhance passenger protection and reliability.

From an infrastructure angle, Hyperloop requires drastically less land in comparison to highways or rail networks. Elevated tubes and streamlined guide structures reduce land usage and environmental disruption. This compact footprint is mainly tremendous in densely populated or environmentally sensitive areas in which expanding conventional transportation infrastructure proves hard.

Moreover, Hyperloop structures promise greater reliability and frequency. Unlike airplanes, which rely heavily on climate conditions and air traffic control, or trains, that can face congestion and scheduling delays, Hyperloop tablets can operate on tightly controlled schedules with speedy departures and arrivals. This ends in progressed punctuality and convenience for passengers.

Comfort and passenger experience additionally gain from Hyperloop's layout. The pods are engineered to reduce vibrations, noise, and surprising actions, providing a smoother experience in comparison to traditional trains or buses. The managed surroundings inside the tubes provides constant temperature and air high-quality, contributing to overall visitor nicely-being.

Finally, the monetary implications of Hyperloop generation are profound. By decreasing travel times and connecting formerly far flung or underserved regions, Hyperloop can stimulate regional development, create new process opportunities, and sell international change. It challenges the repute quo of transportation, compelling industries to innovate and adapt, and paving the way for a greater interconnected and green future.

Hyperloop's advantages over conventional transportation are multi-faceted: it's far quicker, extra energy-efficient, safer, environmentally pleasant, area-saving, reliable, comfortable, and economically transformative. These blended advantages role Hyperloop as a revolutionary step forward in how humanity movements across the land, promising to redefine mobility in the decades to come back.

CHAPTER 2

Working Principles of Hyperloop

2.1. Vacuum Tube System and Air Pressure

One of the important thing components of the Hyperloop technology is the vacuum tube machine, which removes air resistance at some point of travel through casting off as a whole lot air as feasible from the indoors, therefore allowing very excessive speeds to be accomplished. However, for this system to characteristic successfully, the essential physical principles of air pressure and the interactions with the vacuum must be understood, particularly how air strain behaves inside the tube and the way it influences the operation of the device.

The vacuum tube is a core structural thing of the Hyperloop gadget and acts much like a tunnel thru which the transport capsule movements. This tube creates an surroundings this is isolated from the surrounding atmosphere, allowing the tablet to travel at speeds coming near the rate of sound with out the drag forces related to air. For the gadget to function effectively, a particular amount of air must be evacuated from the tube to reap the desired strain tiers, that is essential for the pill's excessive-velocity motion.

The vacuum tube is built the usage of advanced materials consisting of metal, aluminum, and carbon fiber, which are sturdy, lightweight, and durable. These substances help to maintain the low-pressure environment inside the tube. Both ends of the tube are tightly sealed to save you any air leakage, which might disrupt the vacuum and decrease the gadget's performance.

This vacuum environment is vital to minimizing air drag at the tablet, which in flip complements aerodynamic efficiency. However, the usage of a vacuum surroundings also leads to sizeable engineering demanding situations. Specialized structures are required to pump out the air, and every tube should be engineered to prevent leaks that could have an effect on overall performance.

For the vacuum tube device to characteristic properly, the air stress inner ought to be extensively lower than the external atmospheric strain. This reduced air pressure removes tons of the friction that could in any other case obstruct the tablet's motion. Lowering the air strain enables the device to method speeds quicker than sound without encountering the usual aerodynamic drag that might arise at better speeds in a normal atmospheric environment.

Typically, whilst an object attempts to exceed the velocity of sound, it experiences sizeable air resistance due to the high air density. The vacuum surroundings removes this resistance, allowing the tablet to transport greater correctly. This discount in air density also decreases the aerodynamic drag on the pill, which is important for excessive-velocity shipping structures. As a result, much less electricity is required to attain the favored velocities.

In addition, this low-strain surroundings permits the pill to journey quicker and greater correctly, with out the want for traditional friction-based propulsion systems. While this setup gives numerous advantages in terms of velocity, it additionally introduces complicated engineering requirements. Every tube should be sealed meticulously, as any breach may want to lessen performance and create extra mechanical challenges.

Efficient control of air strain is important for the successful operation of the vacuum tube gadget. The inner air strain ought to be kept very low, whilst maintaining secure and cushty situations for passengers. The atmospheric stress out of doors the tube is constantly converting, which means the gadget have to be able to alter to these fluctuations. This requires sophisticated pressure law structures to keep balance within the tube.

Since the stress inside the tube is so low, the air inner should also be conditioned to maintain normal atmospheric conditions for passenger protection and comfort. Without this control, the passengers might be subjected to dangerous conditions. The gadget's ability to dynamically regulate and preserve a low pressure, while ensuring passenger protection, is crucial for long-time period operational fulfillment.

Moreover, outside elements together with gravity, seasonal variations, and weather situations can influence the inner pressure of the tube. Therefore, the machine desires with a view to display and adjust stress stages therefore. These dynamic stress control structures are vital for keeping the performance of the tube and ensuring that the Hyperloop system remains operational over the years.

To enhance the performance of the vacuum tube machine, a selection of recent technology and designs are being advanced. These innovations include micro-sealing systems to prevent air leakage, advanced heating and cooling technologies to optimize power use, and new vacuum pumps that help to hold the low-stress surroundings.

These advancements make the Hyperloop gadget now not simplest faster however additionally more sustainable and environmentally friendly. The ability to eliminate air efficaciously and maintain gold standard stress ranges greatly will increase the energy performance of the device. Furthermore, the improvement of new substances and designs lets in for lighter, more potent, and extra long lasting tubes which are additionally greater eco-friendly.

The vacuum tube device and air strain management are essential to the operation of the Hyperloop. A careful stability of engineering, design, and dynamic manipulate is required for this machine to characteristic efficaciously. By decreasing air resistance and preserving most suitable situations within the tube, the Hyperloop should grow to be one of the maximum green and sustainable modes of transportation within the destiny.

2.2. Electromagnetic Propulsion Systems

Electromagnetic propulsion systems are one of the most progressive and promising technology within the improvement of high-velocity shipping systems like Hyperloop. These systems utilize the standards of electromagnetism to propel a vehicle with out the want for traditional mechanical engines, eliminating friction and reducing power losses. The software of electromagnetic propulsion in the Hyperloop system plays a essential function in attaining the extremely-excessive speeds and electricity performance required for practical, futuristic transportation.

At the core of electromagnetic propulsion lies the interaction between electric and magnetic fields, particularly the phenomenon of electromagnetic induction. When an electric powered present day is exceeded thru a conductor positioned inside a magnetic field, a pressure is generated that could propel the item. This force, called the Lorentz force, acts perpendicular to each the route of the modern-day and the magnetic field, growing movement.

In the Hyperloop system, electromagnetic propulsion makes use of principal principles: magnetic levitation (maglev) and linear synchronous cars (LSM). Both of these strategies depend upon the interplay of electrical currents and magnetic fields to transport the capsule effectively alongside the track or vacuum tube.

Maglev is a era that uses effective magnets to levitate a vehicle above the track, casting off any physical touch between the two. This gets rid of friction, taking into consideration smoother, quicker, and more electricity-green travel. The Hyperloop design consists of a model of maglev technology to raise and stabilize the pill as it actions through the vacuum tube.

In maglev structures, superconducting magnets are frequently used, which offer an exceedingly strong magnetic area with minimal electricity loss. Superconductivity happens while positive materials are cooled to very low temperatures, letting them behavior electricity without resistance. This belongings lets in the magnets to generate vast force with out dropping strength, which is essential for maintaining high speeds and reducing power consumption.

Maglev structures may be categorized into two types: electromagnetic suspension (EMS) and electrodynamic suspension (EDS). EMS makes use of electromagnets to create attractive forces among the automobile and the music, even as EDS makes use of the repulsive force among the automobile's superconducting magnets and the tune's magnetic discipline to levitate the automobile. The choice of which machine to apply inside the Hyperloop relies upon on different factors, which includes cost, efficiency, and operational protection.

Linear synchronous vehicles (LSM) are a key issue of electromagnetic propulsion for structures like Hyperloop.

Unlike traditional electric powered cars, which rotate to create mechanical movement, LSMs generate linear motion via creating a travelling magnetic area that interacts with a sequence of magnets or coils in the car. This form of motor gives several advantages over traditional propulsion strategies, together with excessive efficiency, specific control, and minimal renovation requirements.

In the Hyperloop, the capsule is prepared with everlasting magnets or superconducting coils, whilst the track (or tube) is embedded with a series of electromagnets. When an alternating contemporary passes through those electromagnets, a magnetic subject is created, which moves alongside the duration of the tune. The everlasting magnets or superconducting coils in the tablet are then drawn to or repelled via this magnetic subject, propelling the tablet ahead.

The advantage of the usage of an LSM within the Hyperloop machine is its potential to generate smooth, regular acceleration and deceleration, permitting the pill to reach extraordinarily high speeds with out the jerkiness related to mechanical propulsion systems. Additionally, the LSM machine can function effectively at each excessive and coffee speeds, making it appropriate for the varying wishes of long-distance and town-to-metropolis travel.

Electromagnetic propulsion gives numerous benefits over traditional propulsion systems. The number one benefit is the elimination of friction. With no physical contact between the vehicle and the song, the gadget can operate a whole lot more successfully and with less put on and tear. This appreciably reduces the want for preservation and the electricity losses typically related to friction-based structures.

Another sizeable gain is the potential to reap higher speeds. Since electromagnetic propulsion does no longer depend upon wheels or conventional engines, it is able to theoretically accelerate a automobile to speeds approaching or maybe exceeding the speed of sound. The Hyperloop, with its vacuum tube machine and electromagnetic propulsion, pursuits to reach speeds of as much as 760 mph (1220 km/h), considerably lowering travel time between cities.

Moreover, electromagnetic structures may be greater energy-efficient than conventional strategies. The elimination of friction reduces the general energy required to hold excessive speeds, and the performance of linear cars ensures that greater power is directly translated into movement in place of misplaced as warmth or different forms of electricity waste.

Despite the many advantages of electromagnetic propulsion, there are numerous challenges that need to be addressed for it to turn out to be a sensible and sizeable generation. One of the principle challenges is the excessive fee of developing and maintaining the infrastructure. Maglev and LSM structures require advanced materials, together with superconducting magnets, which can be costly to produce and hold, and the installation of the tune infrastructure is steeply-priced.

Additionally, electromagnetic propulsion structures require specific manipulate to keep away from any misalignment between the capsule and the music. Even small deviations can reason instability, decreasing efficiency and protection. Therefore, the development of exceedingly state-of-the-art steering and manipulate systems is vital to ensure that the Hyperloop remains strong at very excessive speeds.

Another challenge is the requirement for an green cooling system for the superconducting magnets. These magnets need to be cooled to extremely low temperatures, normally using liquid helium, which may be difficult and costly to keep in massive-scale packages. However, advancements in cryogenic technology and more efficient cooling structures are predicted to help deal with those troubles inside the destiny.

As the improvement of Hyperloop and other high-speed transportation systems progresses, the role of electromagnetic propulsion will handiest become extra vast. Continued research into superconducting substances, linear motor technologies, and maglev systems is expected to result in further breakthroughs in efficiency, value discount, and performance.

The integration of electromagnetic propulsion into industrial transportation systems, together with Hyperloop, should revolutionize the way people journey, making lengthy-distance tour quicker, greater green, and greater sustainable. By eliminating the restrictions imposed through conventional propulsion technology, electromagnetic propulsion has the potential to play a major role in shaping the destiny of transportation.

2.3. High Speed and Energy Efficiency

The quest to reap high-velocity tour in structures like Hyperloop is intricately tied to the demanding situations of keeping energy performance. Achieving speeds approaching or exceeding the rate of sound calls for overcoming sizeable technological, engineering, and power-associated hurdles. The performance of a transportation system is crucial, no longer handiest in phrases of lowering running costs however additionally for making sure sustainability inside the face of growing power demands.

High-speed journey provides numerous specific challenges in phrases of power necessities. The faster a vehicle actions, the more power is needed to conquer elements like air resistance, friction, and inertia. In conventional forms of transport together with airplanes or trains, the electricity required to attain high speeds will increase exponentially as pace increases. This dating is referred to as the "dice-square regulation," which dictates that as the scale of a car and its velocity growth, the energy demand grows a lot more considerably.

For instance, in conventional high-speed trains or airplanes, a massive quantity of electricity is used to fight air resistance, which grows with the square of velocity. Additionally, factors including mechanical friction between wheels and rails or engines and gas structures further upload to the energy price. Hyperloop, with its consciousness on overcoming those traditional barriers, is designed to address excessive-pace journey with a lot greater strength efficiency.

One of the center elements of Hyperloop's layout that enables achieve high speeds with lower energy consumption is using a vacuum tube. Unlike conventional sorts of transportation that function in outdoors, Hyperloop drugs will tour thru a low-strain, nearly vacuum surroundings, significantly decreasing the resistance caused by air molecules.

At high speeds, air resistance (drag) will become a primary limiting factor. In conventional excessive-speed transport, this drag will increase dramatically as speed will increase, necessitating extra effective engines to keep speed. However, via lowering the air strain inside the Hyperloop tube, the tablet encounters some distance less drag. This discount lets in the system to maintain high speeds with far much less energy.

The design of the tube additionally incorporates functions that optimize airflow and reduce friction, similarly helping in keeping electricity performance. By lowering resistance on this manner, the Hyperloop machine can attain speeds of up to 760 miles consistent with hour (1220 kilometers in line with hour) even as consuming an awful lot much less electricity as compared to conventional excessive-velocity transportation structures.

As mentioned in advance, Hyperloop makes use of electromagnetic propulsion systems, inclusive of magnetic levitation and linear synchronous motors (LSM), to propel the tablet ahead. These technology are key to accomplishing each high speeds and energy efficiency. By eliminating mechanical friction (such as that which happens in conventional wheel-and-rail systems), the machine can obtain a great deal greater performance in transferring electricity to the automobile.

Traditional propulsion systems depend upon engines that convert gasoline into mechanical energy, with large power loss due to friction, warmness, and other factors. Electromagnetic structures, by assessment, depend on magnetic fields to propel the pill, which leads to an awful lot higher efficiency. The loss of shifting components in the propulsion gadget also reduces the danger of mechanical failure and maintenance needs, in addition reducing electricity consumption and expenses.

Additionally, linear automobiles utilized in Hyperloop systems can provide easy, continuous acceleration and deceleration, making sure that power is used optimally all through the adventure. Unlike conventional structures that can require bursts of energy to triumph over inertia or mechanical resistance, the electromagnetic propulsion machine allows for more controlled and electricity-efficient movement.

Energy performance within the Hyperloop gadget is similarly more desirable with the aid of the use of regenerative braking. In traditional transport systems, braking results inside the dissipation of kinetic power as warmness. However, in electromagnetic systems like Hyperloop, braking may be achieved by reversing the path of the electromagnetic fields, turning the kinetic energy of the automobile returned into usable electrical energy. This energy can then be stored and used to strength the gadget, decreasing universal power consumption.

This regenerative braking system no longer best makes Hyperloop more strength-green however additionally contributes to a more sustainable and green shipping answer. By capturing and reusing energy that would in any other case be lost, Hyperloop's design minimizes waste and maximizes the usage of available strength.

Another critical element in Hyperloop's pursuit of electricity performance is the combination of renewable electricity assets, including sun energy, into the device's infrastructure. Solar panels established on the roofs of Hyperloop stations and along the path can help generate energy to power the device, reducing the dependence on non-renewable power resources.

In a super situation, the strength consumed by using the Hyperloop system would be balanced by the power it generates from sun panels and other renewable sources, growing a self-maintaining, green transportation model. Although attaining whole power independence would require considerable improvements in solar technology and garage potential, the vision for a inexperienced Hyperloop community is a compelling thing of the device's standard layout.

Looking in the direction of the future, Hyperloop's emphasis on excessive-speed and power-green travel holds promise for revolutionizing transportation. In contrast to standard excessive-velocity trains, which devour large amounts of energy to preserve velocity, Hyperloop's aggregate of vacuum technology, electromagnetic propulsion, and regenerative electricity systems represents a prime leap forward in energy performance.

Moreover, the potential to attain speeds of over 700 miles in keeping with hour at the same time as the usage of notably less energy than traditional systems may want to make Hyperloop one of the most sustainable sorts of transportation. The decreased electricity intake and the capability for using renewable power resources are key additives in addressing the environmental challenges associated with conventional delivery systems, which are often heavy customers of fossil fuels.

Hyperloop's design represents an bold and forward-wondering approach to the demanding situations of excessive-speed shipping, supplying a version for the destiny that emphasizes no longer simplest velocity and efficiency but also sustainability and environmental obligation. As the technology maintains to adapt, the potential for even extra strength financial savings and performance upgrades will hold to pressure the improvement of this groundbreaking transportation system.

2.4. Regenerative Braking System

The regenerative braking machine is a critical element of Hyperloop era, gambling a vast role in improving its typical strength performance and sustainability. Unlike traditional braking methods that deplete kinetic strength as warmness through friction, regenerative braking captures this power and converts it returned into usable electrical electricity. This recycled electricity can then be fed again into the device, powering the pods or contributing to the grid, which significantly reduces internet strength consumption during operation.

In the context of Hyperloop, wherein pods travel at noticeably excessive speeds inside vacuum tubes, braking efficaciously and effectively is paramount. The regenerative braking machine is designed to smoothly slow down pods from velocities exceeding 1,000 kilometers in keeping with hour with out depending entirely on mechanical brakes. By the use of electromagnetic forces, the machine applies resistance to the shifting pods, slowing them down whilst concurrently generating electricity. This system minimizes wear and tear on physical additives, extending their lifespan and reducing upkeep charges.

Furthermore, the integration of regenerative braking aligns flawlessly with Hyperloop's emphasis on sustainability. Energy recaptured at some stage in deceleration stages significantly lowers the general power demand, making the machine greater green compared to traditional transportation, which often wastes vast amounts of power in braking strategies. When blended with renewable energy sources that electricity acceleration stages, regenerative braking enables create a close to-self-maintaining transportation loop.

This generation also contributes to the operational efficiency of Hyperloop networks. The capability to successfully recycle power permits extra frequent starts offevolved and stops with out sizable additional energy necessities, helping better throughput and higher scheduling flexibility. Passengers benefit indirectly through reduced operational expenses, that could translate into greater inexpensive fares and tremendous accessibility.

Safety issues are also superior with the aid of regenerative braking. The device offers particular manipulate over deceleration costs, allowing pods to slow down gently and predictably, which improves trip comfort and reduces the threat of mechanical failure. In emergency situations, regenerative braking may be blended with traditional braking methods to make sure speedy but managed stops.

The regenerative braking gadget embodies a middle technological development inside Hyperloop infrastructure. By changing kinetic electricity into electric electricity all through deceleration, it promotes strength conservation, reduces mechanical wear, enhances protection, and helps the overall vision of a fast, green, and environmentally responsible transportation system. This feature isn't always just a technical necessity but a strategic element that allows outline Hyperloop's modern method to trendy mobility.

CHAPTER 3

Hyperloop's Revolution in Transportation

3.1 The Future of Land Transportation

Land transportation has lengthy been a cornerstone of global mobility, assisting monetary activity and private motion. As towns continue to grow, populations boom, and environmental concerns mount, the demand for faster, greater efficient, and extra sustainable varieties of transportation has never been better. The destiny of land transportation is more and more fashioned by improvements inclusive of the Hyperloop, which promises to transform the manner people and goods circulate throughout the planet.

The advent of latest technology, consisting of the Hyperloop, gives the capacity to revolutionize land transportation by means of reducing journey times, growing efficiency, and addressing key challenges related to congestion, pollution, and useful resource intake. Hyperloop, with its vacuum-sealed tubes and electromagnetic propulsion structures, presents an entirely new version for excessive-speed ground tour, offering speeds some distance exceeding those of conventional trains and vehicles. This shift in the direction of quicker, greater green, and sustainable transportation technologies should essentially alternate not simplest how we journey but additionally how we shape towns, regions, and economies.

One of the most on the spot and compelling blessings of Hyperloop era is its capability to drastically reduce journey instances. Traditional land transportation, inclusive of vehicles and trains, operates at speeds limited through the constraints of roads, rail structures, and human factors like driving force fatigue and traffic. Hyperloop, then again, has the potential to exceed the speeds of conventional trains or even airplanes, presenting journey times that are notably shorter. For example, a journey that presently takes several hours by means of vehicle or teach can be finished in a rely of mins, opening up new possibilities for commuting, business tour, and tourism.

The discount in travel times would also have huge consequences on urban making plans and the structure of towns. With high-speed, long-distance land travel, human beings may be capable of stay farther from urban centers whilst nonetheless being able to shuttle correctly for paintings or enjoyment. This could result in the development of recent "city hubs" wherein human beings paintings in one metropolis however live in some other, transforming the nature of urbanization and potentially easing stress on overpopulated metropolitan areas.

Another vital component of the future of land transportation is the increasing need for sustainability. As the arena confronts the fact of weather exchange and environmental degradation, the transportation quarter have to play a imperative role in decreasing carbon emissions and promoting inexperienced technology. Hyperloop generation is positioned as a capability approach to those environmental challenges. By using renewable strength sources and offering more strength performance than traditional transportation strategies, Hyperloop could notably lower the carbon footprint of long-distance tour.

Unlike traditional high-speed trains and airplanes, which rely upon fossil fuels and emit massive portions of greenhouse gases, Hyperloop structures can be powered by way of solar panels, wind strength, or other sustainable resources. This reliance on clean power may want to make Hyperloop a vital part of the worldwide push toward reducing dependence on carbon-based totally fuels and mitigating the environmental effect of transportation. Additionally, using vacuum tubes to reduce air resistance makes Hyperloop extra electricity-green, because the machine can operate at high speeds with less electricity enter.

As the destiny of land transportation moves towards smarter and greater related structures, Hyperloop generation might be incorporated into broader clever mobility solutions. With the increasing use of synthetic intelligence (AI), the Internet of Things (IoT), and advanced facts analytics, transportation systems are becoming greater automatic, optimized, and interconnected. Hyperloop might be a key element of this evolution, running alongside other clever transportation options consisting of independent cars, drones, and smart visitors control systems.

For instance, Hyperloop stations might be seamlessly included into smart town infrastructure, permitting passengers to transport from one mode of transportation to some other with minimal friction. Autonomous motors or electric powered buses should take passengers from Hyperloop stations to their very last destinations, reducing the want for private motors and further lowering congestion in urban areas. Moreover, the combination of AI may want to assist optimize Hyperloop schedules, monitor device performance in actual-time, and ensure that safety protocols are followed robotically, reducing the threat of injuries or delays.

Land transportation structures, especially the ones in foremost urban facilities, are an increasing number of strained by using population growth and growing demand for mobility. Traffic congestion, long commute times, and the environmental fees of conventional transportation are becoming giant troubles in towns worldwide. Hyperloop should alleviate some of these issues by providing an alternative mode of shipping that operates outside of congested roadways and concrete infrastructures.

By supplying high-pace travel between towns, Hyperloop may want to reduce the want for lengthy-distance car journey, thereby lowering traffic on highways and interstates. The system may also help mitigate the outcomes of city sprawl by using making it simpler for humans to stay in suburban or rural regions at the same time as nonetheless getting access to the monetary and cultural opportunities available in huge cities. This decoupling of wherein human beings stay and work may want to alternate the panorama of cities and regions, developing more balanced urbanization styles and decreasing the pressures on crowded metropolitan areas.

The upward push of Hyperloop ought to disrupt present transportation industries, specifically those focused on rail, aviation, and car sectors. The capacity for quicker, more efficient journey should make contemporary techniques of transportation appear previous, in particular for long-distance journeys. This disruption ought to pressure innovation throughout the industry, forcing traditional players to evolve or lose marketplace percentage to new technology.

For instance, airlines ought to face stiff competition from Hyperloop for short to medium-variety routes. While airplanes are perfect for international tour, Hyperloop could provide a extra fee-effective and environmentally friendly alternative for domestic and nearby routes. Similarly, the car enterprise is probably affected as fewer human beings rely on non-public motors for lengthy-distance journey, opting as an alternative for excessive-velocity, excessive-efficiency Hyperloop journeys.

As these industries adjust to the brand new competitive panorama, we may want to see further investments in complementary technology that improve the overall efficiency and sustainability of land-primarily based transportation, paving the manner for a extra incorporated and diversified transportation surroundings.

3.2 The Transformation of Intercity Travel

Intercity journey has constantly been an essential aspect of contemporary lifestyles, connecting areas, economies, and cultures. Whether for enterprise, amusement, or migration, visiting between towns has shaped societal structures and global dynamics. However, conventional modes of transportation, which includes trains, buses, and cars, are frequently plagued through boundaries in speed, efficiency, and environmental sustainability. Hyperloop technology guarantees to revolutionize intercity tour, presenting a jump ahead in pace, convenience, and sustainability, and fundamentally altering how human beings circulate throughout big distances.

The transformation of intercity journey thru Hyperloop era may be visible in numerous key regions: speed, accessibility, value-effectiveness, and environmental impact. Hyperloop's capacity to redefine the manner humans travel among towns isn't just about faster travel instances however additionally about converting the complete travel experience, allowing more seamless, sustainable, and interconnected trips.

One of the most transformative aspects of Hyperloop technology is its ability to considerably reduce journey times among cities. Conventional varieties of intercity transportation, together with high-velocity trains, buses, and cars, often take several hours or maybe an afternoon to cowl distances that Hyperloop should make in a fraction of the time. For example, tour between major towns that currently takes hours through train or automobile should potentially be decreased to mere minutes, fundamentally changing how humans consider the distances among them.

Hyperloop structures may want to make lengthy-distance journey between neighboring cities as brief as a short commute, beginning up new possibilities for local improvement, economic collaboration, and private mobility. For example, cities which can be several hundred miles aside will be connected in underneath an hour, permitting human beings to travel across areas with unheard of velocity and performance. This could create a brand new technology of "commuter towns," wherein people should live in a single metropolis at the same time as working or studying in another, reshaping city and nearby making plans.

The pace of Hyperloop systems could also advantage industries that rely on speedy motion of goods and services. The ability to move goods quick among towns would beautify the efficiency of logistics networks and decrease transport instances, probably enhancing deliver chain management and boosting the worldwide economic system.

The introduction of Hyperloop could appreciably beautify the accessibility of regions that have been previously difficult or high-priced to attain. Today, many towns are constrained by their distance from principal transportation hubs, making tour to and from them time-ingesting and costly. Hyperloop, with its community of vacuum-sealed tubes connecting multiple towns, could permit for greater equitable get admission to to transportation, even for smaller cities and rural areas that were once underserved by conventional transportation structures.

By connecting those areas to important urban centers, Hyperloop may want to open up new possibilities for financial boom and social mobility. People living in smaller towns should greater effortlessly get right of entry to jobs, education, and services in larger cities, leading to extra monetary integration. In turn, essential cities ought to benefit from the inflow of recent skills, resources, and ideas, further stimulating monetary improvement and innovation.

Hyperloop's capacity to shorten journey times between cities could result in the introduction of economic corridors, in which areas with complementary industries may want to thrive via replacing items, services, and know-how with extra ease. For example, towns focusing on production, generation, or studies ought to gain from faster and greater green collaboration with neighboring regions, in the long run growing a greater incorporated worldwide economy.

Another massive advantage of Hyperloop technology is its capacity to offer a greater price-powerful and sustainable opportunity to current intercity tour methods. High-velocity trains, airplanes, and motors are regularly related to excessive running fees, vast environmental effect, and constrained accessibility. In evaluation, Hyperloop guarantees a extra efficient, strength-green, and environmentally pleasant solution.

Unlike air tour, which is predicated on fossil fuels and is a major contributor to carbon emissions, Hyperloop structures can be powered with the aid of renewable electricity sources, which include solar or wind power, significantly lowering their carbon footprint. The use of vacuum-sealed tubes also minimizes air resistance, making Hyperloop more electricity-efficient than conventional styles of transportation, which require a constant supply of strength to overcome friction and resistance.

The pretty low running expenses of Hyperloop may want to make intercity travel extra low priced for a much wider variety of people. With lower fares as compared to conventional trains and planes, Hyperloop ought to democratize tour, allowing more human beings to get entry to faster, more reliable transportation. This could have a profound impact on mobility, making intercity journey more inclusive and accessible for human beings from all walks of life.

Hyperloop ought to redefine the passenger enjoy via imparting a faster, smoother, and greater cushty alternative to conventional intercity transportation. Unlike airplanes or trains, which regularly involve lengthy ready instances, safety checks, and crowded stations, Hyperloop stations can be designed to provide a unbroken and green tour revel in. Passengers could check in and board quick, with minimal delays or interruptions, ensuring a smoother normal journey.

The design of Hyperloop pods, which journey in vacuum tubes, also promises to offer a quieter and greater snug ride. The absence of air resistance approach less noise and vibration, developing a more pleasant environment for passengers. The easy, high-speed tour revel in can be akin to the comfort and comfort of air travel but with the delivered gain of a greater green and cost-effective mode of transport.

Moreover, Hyperloop structures could offer passengers with more flexibility and comfort in terms of scheduling and routes. Instead of counting on constant timetables and routes, passengers may want to select from various travel alternatives that quality in shape their needs, taking into account extra customized and dynamic travel plans. This flexibility should make intercity journey more adaptable to the fast-paced needs of current existence.

As Hyperloop technology continues to increase, it may facilitate the introduction of an interconnected worldwide transportation network, similarly improving intercity tour on a worldwide scale. Hyperloop could turn out to be a key part of an included transportation device that links distinct international locations and continents, lowering boundaries to worldwide mobility and fostering greater cultural trade and cooperation.

For instance, Hyperloop structures ought to eventually be prolonged to go-border connections, taking into account brief and efficient travel between towns in distinct countries. This should promote worldwide tourism, change, and collaboration, fostering a greater interconnected international. The potential to travel among important cities in different areas effortlessly should create new possibilities for cultural change, scientific cooperation, and monetary integration on a worldwide scale.

Hyperloop's capacity to reshape intercity tour isn't simply confined to improving the rate and performance of transportation. By connecting people and areas in new methods, Hyperloop should alternate the way we live, work, and interact with each other, growing a more interconnected, sustainable, and on hand international for future generations.

3.3 Time and Cost Savings in Transportation

One of the most compelling benefits of Hyperloop technology is its capability to provide great time and fee financial savings within the transportation quarter. As the call for for quicker, more green journey grows globally, the

Hyperloop promises to cope with these needs by means of notably lowering travel instances while imparting a more price-powerful alternative to conventional transportation techniques. The implications of those benefits are some distance-reaching, impacting not handiest person vacationers but additionally agencies, economies, and the environment.

Hyperloop era promises to redefine how we perceive tour time. Traditional types of transportation, such as high-pace trains, airplanes, and motors, can take hours to cover distances that Hyperloop ought to potentially entire in a fragment of the time. For example, the 400-mile journey between towns that could presently take several hours by using educate or vehicle might be decreased to just 30 minutes with Hyperloop, and even air tour would see a good sized reduction in tour time. This bounce in speed could basically trade how people view intercity and go-u. S. A. Tour.

The reduction in journey time could significantly beautify productivity by using allowing people to spend much less time commuting and greater time focusing on work, enjoyment, or other crucial activities. For agencies, quicker transportation way faster get admission to to markets, sources, and talent pools. It can also make it less complicated for people to tour for work with out taking prolonged periods of break day, facilitating a greater dynamic and connected worldwide team of workers.

Moreover, Hyperloop may want to permit identical-day tour among towns that are currently tough to attain inside a single day. This flexibility might be particularly tremendous for organizations that rely upon frequent journey for meetings, conferences, or different time-touchy sports, leading to an increase in each private and expert possibilities. The ability to tour throughout regions or even countries within hours instead of days may want to spark new innovations in business fashions, creating efficiencies that had been previously not possible.

In addition to time financial savings, Hyperloop guarantees to provide a greater fee-powerful transportation alternative compared to traditional strategies. Currently, excessive-pace trains, airplanes, and long-distance car journey include giant prices. Air tour, for instance, entails gas costs, maintenance, and operational overhead, while excessive-pace trains require high-priced infrastructure investments and ongoing subsidies. Hyperloop, via contrast, is designed to be a greater green and sustainable mode of shipping that would decrease common operational fees.

The electricity performance of Hyperloop era is one of the key elements contributing to its potential for price savings. Unlike airplanes, which rely on jet gas and create full-size greenhouse fuel emissions, Hyperloop structures might be powered with the aid of renewable strength assets, including solar or wind energy, making the operation of Hyperloop an awful lot extra price-powerful and environmentally sustainable.

Furthermore, the use of vacuum tubes considerably reduces air resistance, allowing Hyperloop pods to travel with minimal electricity expenditure. This energy efficiency can be handed directly to clients inside the form of lower fares.

The cost savings could now not be restricted to the passengers on my own. The discount in operational fees may want to make Hyperloop a viable alternative for transporting items and load, in addition decreasing logistics prices and boosting deliver chain efficiency. With reduced transportation charges, agencies ought to see lower transport costs, leading to less expensive goods and services for clients. The savings across a couple of sectors could stimulate monetary boom by way of making it less complicated to conduct business, facilitate alternate, and improve get right of entry to to assets.

In addition to time and direct economic savings, Hyperloop can also yield extensive environmental blessings. Traditional transportation techniques—particularly air travel and long-distance trucking—contribute closely to greenhouse gas emissions, air pollution, and environmental degradation. Hyperloop's power-green design and capacity use of clean power sources could greatly lessen its carbon footprint, offering a greater sustainable opportunity that could assist mitigate the environmental effect of transportation.

The infrastructure required for Hyperloop systems, even though enormous, could prove to be extra value-powerful over the years as compared to high-velocity rail or airport improvement. Building new airports or increasing current ones requires full-size capital investment, no longer best for creation but also for ongoing preservation and staffing. Similarly, excessive-speed rail networks require widespread music construction, electrification, and maintenance. Hyperloop, by means of comparison, relies on a exceedingly less complicated infrastructure of vacuum-sealed tubes and stations, that may reduce long-term expenses, in particular if incorporated into current delivery corridors or urban traits.

Moreover, Hyperloop systems can be built in areas where conventional infrastructure might not be viable, including densely populated urban environments or regions with difficult terrain. The modularity of Hyperloop generation lets in for greater flexible integration into current city and suburban landscapes, doubtlessly reducing the want for luxurious and disruptive creation projects. This adaptability may want to bring about great savings for governments and private organizations making an investment in transportation infrastructure.

The time and value financial savings facilitated by using Hyperloop could have a ripple impact at some point of the global economic system. The capacity to quickly and cheaply join cities and regions ought to result in extended monetary pastime via beginning up new markets, growing jobs, and allowing more green trade. Hyperloop's ability to reduce transportation expenses and travel times could assist boom the flow of products, services, and people, leading to more economic integration among cities, areas, or even international locations.

For example, companies ought to operate greater efficaciously by way of gaining access to a much broader skills pool and having a broader customer base inside the attain of only a few hours of travel. In addition, tourism and enjoyment tour could see a vast boost, as humans would be more inclined to go to towns and nations previously taken into consideration too distant or expensive to attain. The elevated drift of human beings and goods should drive activity advent, infrastructure improvement, and innovation, in the end benefiting economies on a neighborhood, national, and global scale.

As Hyperloop becomes a fact, the indirect financial effect could be transformative, main to new industries, better get entry to to training and healthcare, and a greater connected international community. The potential for big economic boom, coupled with environmental blessings and stepped forward best of life, makes Hyperloop a promising investment for the destiny.

The lengthy-time period blessings of time and cost financial savings supplied via Hyperloop could be found out throughout multiple sectors, from transportation to logistics, tourism, or even healthcare. The ability to transport people and goods quickly and cost effectively might revolutionize industries that depend upon speedy movement and accessibility. With time now not a widespread barrier, groups could innovate quicker, human beings ought to work throughout borders, and international collaboration ought to attain extraordinary tiers.

As Hyperloop technology matures and expands, its large adoption may want to result in big savings throughout both non-public and public sectors, making it a cornerstone of the destiny of transportation. From reducing journey instances for ordinary commuters to fostering more financial cooperation and improvement, the long-time period effect of Hyperloop might be felt via generations to return.

3.4. Impact on Urban and Regional Connectivity

The creation of Hyperloop technology guarantees to dramatically reshape city and local connectivity, revolutionizing the way towns and surrounding regions have interaction and function. Traditional transportation infrastructures regularly restriction the benefit and velocity with which people and items move among city centers and their peripheral regions, leading to congestion, financial disparities, and inefficient land use. Hyperloop's extraordinary pace and performance have the potential to break down those barriers, fostering greater included, dynamic, and resilient urban ecosystems.

One of the maximum profound influences of Hyperloop on connectivity is the redefinition of what constitutes a possible commuting distance. By enabling journey speeds exceeding 1,000 kilometers in keeping with hour, Hyperloop can reduce journeys that traditionally take numerous hours by way of automobile or educate to mere mins. This compression of travel time correctly expands metropolitan regions, allowing citizens to live further from town centers with out sacrificing accessibility to jobs, training, and cultural amenities. The end result is the introduction of huge "mega-areas" in which monetary and social activities drift seamlessly throughout previously separated city and suburban zones.

This new connectivity additionally encourages balanced regional development. Instead of overburdening essential city hubs with populace growth and site visitors congestion, Hyperloop facilitates the dispersal of financial interest across a broader geographic area. Smaller towns and towns turn out to be more appealing as places to live and paintings, benefiting from improved access to large markets and assets. This decentralization can lessen the pressure on urban infrastructure, lower housing fees in overcrowded towns, and stimulate investments in underdeveloped areas.

From a logistical perspective, Hyperloop offers a transformative benefit for freight and deliver chain control inside and between city regions. Fast, dependable, and strength-efficient motion of products can lessen delivery times and prices, growing the competitiveness of regional economies. Moreover, with the aid of alleviating the dependence on road freight, Hyperloop can lessen site visitors congestion and pollutants in cities, contributing to more healthy, extra livable city environments.

Integration with present transportation networks amplifies Hyperloop's effect on connectivity. By connecting seamlessly with nearby public transit, high-velocity rail, and airports, Hyperloop serves as a backbone for multimodal tour, making sure that passengers experience clean transitions across special transportation modes. This holistic connectivity reduces journey friction, encouraging extra use of public and sustainable transport options.

However, the expansion of connectivity also brings challenges. Rapid modifications in populace distribution may require new city making plans techniques to manipulate land use, environmental effect, and social fairness. Ensuring that all communities benefit similarly from superior connectivity is critical to save you widening socioeconomic divides.

Hyperloop technology has the power to redefine city and local landscapes with the aid of linking towns and their hinterlands in methods formerly unattainable. It promotes greater accessibility, monetary vitality, and environmental sustainability, paving the manner for smarter, greater connected regions that may better meet the challenges of the 21st century.

3.5. Disrupting Existing Transportation Industries

Hyperloop era is poised to basically disrupt current transportation industries by way of challenging the established norms of velocity, efficiency, fee, and sustainability. Traditional sectors which includes railways, automobile, and aviation face unprecedented opposition as Hyperloop introduces a appreciably new paradigm in how people and items flow over land. This disruption consists of sizeable implications now not best for marketplace dynamics but additionally for regulatory frameworks, exertions markets, and infrastructure funding priorities global.

Firstly, Hyperloop's potential to attain speeds a long way exceeding those of conventional trains and vehicles threatens to render many present day modes of transport obsolete or much less competitive for intercity tour. High-pace rail networks, which have long been taken into consideration the pinnacle of land transportation innovation, might also war to compete with Hyperloop's extensively reduced tour instances and operational expenses. Similarly, vehicle travel over medium distances—commutes that historically span one to numerous hours—should dramatically decline as passengers opt for Hyperloop's speedy and cushty alternatives.

The aviation industry, specially domestic and quick-haul flights, additionally faces main disruption. Hyperloop's travel times for distances as much as several hundred kilometers can rival or beat those of airplanes whilst factoring in airport check-in, security, boarding, and taxiing times. Additionally, Hyperloop gives environmental benefits over air journey, that's increasingly scrutinized for its carbon emissions. As sustainability worries intensify, governments and clients may additionally shift choices towards Hyperloop, incentivizing airways to evolve or refocus their services.

The ripple outcomes make bigger to freight and logistics as properly. Hyperloop's speedy and reliable cargo shipping talents may want to disrupt trucking and rail freight sectors by way of supplying a purifier, greater green alternative. This shift has the potential to regulate supply chains, lessen motorway congestion, and decrease put on and tear on avenue infrastructure.

However, disruption does no longer arise with out demanding situations. Existing transportation industries represent deeply entrenched interests with significant monetary and political have an impact on. Resistance to change, regulatory hurdles, and the high capital prices related to building Hyperloop infrastructure may additionally slow adoption. Moreover, team of workers transitions pose social demanding situations, as jobs tied to standard shipping modes ought to decline, necessitating retraining and coverage interventions to manage employment shifts.

From a regulatory perspective, Hyperloop introduces new complexities. Existing laws and protection requirements, designed round set up technologies, will want to be reevaluated and improved to house the unique operational characteristics of vacuum tubes, electromagnetic propulsion, and automatic controls. Collaboration among governments, industry stakeholders, and worldwide our bodies may be vital to craft frameworks that balance innovation with public safety and fairness.

On the investment front, the emergence of Hyperloop is driving sizeable capital flows into studies, improvement, and infrastructure projects. This influx of resources may want to boost up innovation cycles and foster new enterprise fashions, which includes public-private partnerships and incorporated mobility systems. Traditional transportation businesses may additionally locate possibilities to pivot with the aid of investing in or collaborating with Hyperloop ventures, reworking potential disruption into strategic evolution.

Hyperloop represents a disruptive force reshaping the transportation panorama throughout multiple dimensions. It challenges the rate, fee, environmental impact, and comfort of current modes, while compelling industries and policymakers to reconsider the future of mobility. The transition to a Hyperloop-enabled world will certainly be complicated but gives big potential to create a faster, cleaner, and extra linked worldwide transportation ecosystem.

CHAPTER 4

Environmental Impacts of Hyperloop

4.1. Carbon Footprint and Sustainability

As the global network grapples with the growing demanding situations of weather exchange and environmental degradation, transportation remains one in all the biggest individuals to carbon emissions. The pursuit of sustainable and electricity-efficient transportation technologies has therefore emerge as a important vicinity of innovation. Among the most promising of these innovations is the Hyperloop, a high-velocity transportation device that pursuits to revolutionize the manner people and goods flow. The environmental effect of Hyperloop, specially in terms of its carbon footprint and sustainability, plays a primary position in determining its capability to reshape international transportation.

Before delving into the capacity environmental advantages of Hyperloop, it's far crucial to recognize the carbon footprint related to conventional transportation methods. The transportation quarter is accountable for a vast element of world greenhouse gas emissions, broadly speaking thru the use of fossil fuels in cars, vans, trains, and airplanes. According to the International Energy Agency (IEA), transportation accounts for kind of 25% of worldwide power-associated CO_2 emissions, with road automobiles making up the biggest percentage. Aviation, whilst a smaller area in phrases of emissions, has a disproportionately excessive effect due to the electricity depth of lengthy-haul flights.

In addition to $CO2$ emissions, conventional transportation systems also contribute to air pollution, noise pollutants, and the consumption of non-renewable sources. Fossil gasoline dependency and the environmental prices related to the extraction, refinement, and combustion of oil and fuel make the modern-day transportation infrastructure unsustainable within the long term.

The Hyperloop machine is designed with the intention of substantially decreasing the carbon footprint of transportation. At its middle, Hyperloop is based on electric propulsion and operates within a close to-vacuum surroundings that minimizes air resistance, enabling motors to journey at speeds exceeding 700 miles in keeping with hour (1,100 km/h). The streamlined layout of the pods, combined with the efficiency of the vacuum tube, leads to noticeably decrease electricity consumption as compared to standard excessive-velocity trains, airplanes, and other sorts of transportation.

One of the primary approaches in which Hyperloop can lessen its carbon footprint is thru its reliance on renewable power sources. The gadget is estimated to be powered ordinarily via solar power, with sun panels hooked up alongside the duration of the tubes to harness daylight and generate strength. This might make the device in large part self-sustaining, as the power generated from solar panels couldn't simplest power the Hyperloop pods but additionally the entire infrastructure, along with the stations and auxiliary structures. By tapping into renewable energy, Hyperloop has the potential to significantly reduce its reliance on fossil fuels and decrease the carbon emissions related to the transportation manner.

Furthermore, the ability to apply sun energy in an incorporated manner approach that the system could be carbon-impartial or even carbon-terrible, relying at the quantity to which extra power is generated and stored. As the generation matures, it is able to pave the manner for a global shift toward carbon-unfastened transportation networks, contributing significantly to the fight against weather exchange.

The environmental benefits of Hyperloop are not constrained to its operational segment. The complete lifecycle of the machine, from construction to decommissioning, will have an effect on its typical sustainability. The construction of Hyperloop infrastructure, which include the vacuum tubes, stations, and propulsion systems, calls for sizeable substances, power, and hard work. It is crucial to assess the carbon footprint of these substances and the electricity used in the course of the development segment to assess the proper sustainability of the machine.

However, a key advantage of the Hyperloop layout is its extraordinarily low land use in comparison to conventional transportation structures. The creation of highways, railroads, and airports requires extensive quantities of land, regularly ensuing in deforestation, habitat destruction, and disruption of ecosystems. In contrast, the Hyperloop machine might be constructed above floor on accelerated tracks or below floor in tunnels, minimizing its effect on the encircling environment. The compact and green design of Hyperloop stations also reduces the need for expansive infrastructure, further retaining treasured land sources.

Additionally, due to the fact the Hyperloop is designed to be a modular gadget, it allows for smooth growth and flexibility with out the want for constant rebuilding or expansion of infrastructure. This no longer best reduces the environmental price of ongoing construction however additionally enables a extra flexible approach to meeting growing transportation needs in a sustainable manner.

While the environmental capacity of Hyperloop is substantial, there are nonetheless several demanding situations and considerations to cope with with a view to fully comprehend its sustainability dreams. One of the main demanding situations lies in the manufacturing and disposal of substances used in the production of the system. For instance, the production of metallic, concrete, and other materials wanted for the vacuum tubes and infrastructure is energy-in depth and contributes to carbon emissions. Developing new, sustainable materials and decreasing the carbon footprint of production techniques will be vital in ensuring that Hyperloop stays an environmentally possible answer.

Another consideration is the long-time period environmental effect of electricity storage and battery technology. While renewable power sources like sun strength can provide the important power for the device, power garage solutions might be required to ensure regular operation, in particular in the course of durations of low daylight or whilst call for spikes. Developing green and sustainable energy garage structures, together with superior battery technology or different kinds of strength garage, may be key to preserving the environmental integrity of the device over the years.

Additionally, the potential environmental influences of the substances and technology used inside the manufacturing of Hyperloop automobiles and infrastructure need to be cautiously assessed. For example, the rare earth substances required for the construction of sure components, including superconducting magnets for the propulsion gadget, have to be sourced sustainably. Mining operations for these substances could have vast environmental effects if no longer managed properly. Ensuring that the supply chain for Hyperloop's additives is both moral and environmentally responsible may be critical in mitigating the machine's ordinary ecological effect.

Hyperloop has the capacity to play a transformative function in international sustainability desires, particularly in addressing transportation-related emissions and decreasing reliance on fossil fuels. The United Nations' Sustainable Development Goals (SDGs) emphasize the importance of sustainable cities and groups, low cost and easy energy, and weather movement. Hyperloop's integration into modern-day transportation networks ought to make contributions at once to those objectives by means of presenting a smooth, electricity-efficient alternative to traditional methods of journey.

By appreciably decreasing transportation-related emissions and minimizing strength consumption, Hyperloop should come to be a cornerstone of sustainable mobility, assisting the transition to a low-carbon financial system. Moreover, its potential to connect cities and areas extra effectively, with reduced environmental expenses, aligns with the global trend of urbanization and the need for sustainable infrastructure solutions. By reducing the need for avenue and air tour, Hyperloop can also alleviate site visitors congestion and reduce the stress on existing transportation systems, in addition contributing to environmental sustainability.

Hyperloop represents an exciting and innovative option to the environmental challenges of modern transportation. Its potential to reduce carbon emissions, make use of renewable strength sources, and limit its land footprint gives a promising direction closer to sustainable transportation networks. However, the successful consciousness of these blessings will rely on overcoming engineering, fabric, and logistical demanding situations, particularly in phrases of production and energy garage.

While it's far still inside the early ranges of development, the promise of a carbon-neutral or even carbon-poor transportation gadget positions Hyperloop as a potential recreation-changer inside the worldwide attempt to combat weather alternate. By addressing environmental worries and presenting a sustainable alternative to standard modes of transportation, Hyperloop should redefine the destiny of journey, contributing to a cleaner, greener planet for destiny generations.

4.2. Efficient Use of Natural Resources

As the arena faces the urgent need to reduce its environmental effect and embody sustainable practices, the green use of herbal sources has come to be a key consideration inside the development of present day technology. Hyperloop, a promising new transportation device, offers great ability for using natural assets extra correctly as compared to conventional modes of transportation.

One of the principal tenets of Hyperloop technology is its ability for electricity efficiency. The system is designed to decrease power intake via its streamlined operation. Unlike traditional transportation methods, which rely upon friction-heavy mechanisms including wheels on tracks or jet engines that burn fuel, Hyperloop's layout minimizes friction by way of the use of a close to-vacuum surroundings in the tubes. The lack of air resistance and the decreased friction between the vehicle and the music method that much less energy is wanted to reap and keep excessive speeds. This essential layout function considerably reduces the quantity of strength required to transport passengers and cargo, making it a long way more efficient than modern-day transport options.

Moreover, Hyperloop is expected to depend closely on renewable power resources, mainly solar strength. Solar panels mounted alongside the duration of the Hyperloop tune can harness daylight to generate strength. In a really perfect setup, the quantity of electricity produced through solar panels could not handiest strength the Hyperloop machine however also offer surplus strength to be fed lower back into the grid. This sustainable strength supply would lessen the reliance on fossil fuels, reducing the environmental impact and promoting a extra accountable use of natural assets.

The use of renewable power also guarantees that the general carbon footprint of the Hyperloop device remains minimum, contributing to the renovation of herbal assets and lowering the depletion of non-renewable electricity resources which includes coal, oil, and herbal fuel. By supplying a possible opportunity to fossil fuel-powered transportation, Hyperloop could play a key role in global efforts to lessen electricity intake and shift closer to a more sustainable energy infrastructure.

The substances utilized in constructing the Hyperloop infrastructure also play a substantial position in its environmental effect. Traditional transportation structures, such as roads, railways, and airports, eat widespread quantities of herbal sources in their creation. Hyperloop objectives to decrease material consumption thru its progressive design and creation strategies, promoting sustainable material usage.

For instance, the development of Hyperloop tubes calls for high-strength materials, however the layout seeks to apply substances that are each lightweight and durable. Lightweight substances reduce the need for immoderate structural reinforcement and decrease the overall power required for transportation. Additionally, the efficient layout of the gadget way that fewer materials may be required within the creation section, decreasing the stress on natural resources.

The development of latest, more sustainable substances additionally plays a essential function within the long-time period viability of the machine. For instance, advanced composites and different progressive materials which might be lighter, stronger, and more environmentally pleasant are being explored for Hyperloop infrastructure. These materials no longer handiest reduce the carbon footprint during the development section however also make sure that the device remains resilient and efficient over the years, extending the existence cycle of the infrastructure and minimizing the need for frequent upkeep or replacements.

In terms of automobile creation, Hyperloop pods are designed to be smooth and efficient, with a minimalistic method to additives. By decreasing the quantity of components and materials involved in the vehicles' design, Hyperloop can further make a contribution to the sustainable use of assets.

In addition to energy and materials, land use is some other essential attention whilst evaluating the sustainability of transportation structures. Traditional infrastructure inclusive of highways, railways, and airports requires vast amounts of land, regularly leading to the destruction of natural habitats, deforestation, and other environmental disruptions. In assessment, Hyperloop's design permits for a extra efficient use of land, reducing the ecological footprint associated with transportation infrastructure.

Hyperloop structures can be constructed above floor on improved tracks, which minimizes the need to clean massive regions of land for creation. By raising the device, Hyperloop avoids conflicts with current land uses and preserves the encircling environment. Additionally, the compact layout of Hyperloop stations and terminals reduces the amount of area wanted for the device, making it less complicated to integrate into present urban landscapes without eating big quantities of land or contributing to city sprawl.

Alternatively, Hyperloop may be constructed underground, in addition lowering the environmental effect by way of keeping off the need for expansive floor-stage infrastructure. Underground systems could have minimal interaction with natural ecosystems and could lessen the want for land acquisition, making it simpler to combine Hyperloop into densely populated urban regions.

The efficient use of land also contributes to the device's financial viability. With much less land required for infrastructure, the fee of creation may be diminished, and more flexible alternatives for urban making plans and development grow to be to be had. By preserving natural landscapes and lowering the want for huge-scale land adjustments, Hyperloop gives a more sustainable and green method to transportation infrastructure.

Another thing of resource use in Hyperloop's design is its management of water assets and waste. As Hyperloop structures perform with near-vacuum situations and minimum mechanical friction, they're much less probable to generate the environmental pollution generally related to transportation systems, consisting of water runoff, waste, or hazardous emissions. Because the technology is based on a closed-loop system, the amount of waste generated all through operation is minimized, in addition lowering the environmental footprint.

Moreover, the capacity for Hyperloop to be powered through sun strength and other renewable sources reduces the need for water-in depth strength era methods, together with coal or nuclear strength flora. These strength resources, which usually require widespread water for cooling, make a contribution to the depletion of nearby water assets. By using sustainable strength resources, Hyperloop avoids those bad influences, contributing to the conservation of water.

The efficient use of herbal resources is a cornerstone of Hyperloop's capacity for a sustainable destiny. By prioritizing strength efficiency, sustainable material utilization, land conservation, and minimizing the effect on water sources, Hyperloop can set a new preferred for transportation generation. Its ability to reduce the reliance on fossil fuels, optimize resource intake, and limit environmental disruptions positions it as a key participant in the worldwide transition to a more sustainable and environmentally accountable future. Hyperloop represents a soar forward in how we reflect onconsideration on aid use in transportation, with the ability to inspire new techniques throughout industries and sectors.

4.3. The Environmental Impact of Advanced Technologies

As the arena increasingly more turns to superior technology to cope with transportation challenges, it's far vital to bear in mind not simplest their capacity blessings but also their environmental effect. While innovations just like the Hyperloop promise huge advancements in pace, efficiency, and sustainability, their broader environmental results should be carefully assessed.

One of the most widespread environmental advantages of Hyperloop technology lies in its capacity to reduce energy intake. Traditional modes of transportation, which include cars, trains, and airplanes, depend heavily on fossil fuels, contributing to air pollution, carbon emissions, and the depletion of non-renewable resources. Hyperloop, however, is designed to be energy-efficient and is predicted to run on renewable power sources which includes solar strength. This shift to renewable energy is a important step toward reducing the environmental footprint of transportation systems.

The layout of the Hyperloop machine minimizes strength waste through using a vacuum tube that drastically reduces air resistance, permitting motors to tour at high speeds with much less energy enter. Additionally, Hyperloop infrastructure is probably to be powered by means of sun panels mounted alongside the tracks, potentially producing more power than the machine consumes. This surplus strength could be fed back into the grid, making Hyperloop a net contributor to smooth strength manufacturing.

By counting on renewable energy, Hyperloop has the capacity to significantly decrease the carbon emissions associated with tour, making it a miles greater sustainable option as compared to traditional delivery strategies. However, the lengthy-time period environmental effect of electricity intake will depend upon the full-size availability and adoption of renewable strength, in addition to the potential to preserve electricity performance because the device scales.

The creation of any big-scale transportation system calls for massive resources, both in terms of uncooked materials and electricity. However, Hyperloop has been designed to optimize aid usage, decreasing its environmental effect during the development phase. Traditional transportation infrastructure, together with highways and railways, often consumes massive amounts of land, steel, concrete, and other raw substances. Hyperloop, with its glossy, increased layout, minimizes the need for good sized land change and decreases the quantity of materials required for its production.

In particular, lightweight, high-energy substances are a key feature of Hyperloop's design. By utilizing advanced composites and other innovative substances, Hyperloop minimizes the structural weight of the gadget, lowering the electricity had to shipping both passengers and cargo. This material performance is important for the sustainability of the system, as it helps to lessen the general environmental footprint of its creation.

Furthermore, the efficiency of the substances utilized in Hyperloop's production can contribute to the toughness of the infrastructure. Unlike conventional shipping structures which could require frequent repairs or rebuilding, Hyperloop's use of durable substances may amplify the lifespan of the gadget and reduce the want for aid-in depth maintenance.

Hyperloop's layout also minimizes the generation of waste and harmful emissions. Conventional transportation structures produce quite a number environmental pollution, together with exhaust emissions from vehicles and airplanes, noise pollutants from trains, and the warmth generated by way of street networks. Hyperloop, but, operates in a controlled, sealed environment that reduces the potential for pollution.

Because the system is based on electromagnetic propulsion and a vacuum tube, it is unfastened from the mechanical friction that generates warmness, noise, and emissions in traditional structures. The electromagnetic pressure is rather efficient and produces little to no waste during operation. Additionally, Hyperloop stations and infrastructure will probably incorporate waste control systems that minimize environmental damage, further reducing the system's ecological footprint.

One of the fundamental environmental worries associated with transportation structures is their effect on ecosystems and flora and fauna. Roads, railways, and airports frequently require huge amounts of land, leading to habitat destruction, deforestation, and disruption of wildlife migration styles.

Hyperloop, however, has been designed with the purpose of minimizing those disruptions.

The elevated design of Hyperloop tubes way that lots of the system can be constructed above ground, allowing it to avoid disrupting ecosystems which can be positioned on the floor. By using existing urban infrastructure and integrating the gadget into already-developed areas, Hyperloop can reduce the need for brand new land acquisition and decrease the environmental impact on untouched herbal habitats.

Additionally, Hyperloop's creation will probably awareness on regions where human improvement already exists, along with transportation corridors or urbanized regions, reducing the need to encroach on covered landscapes or ecologically touchy regions. This cautious attention of land use will assist keep ecosystems and prevent the environmental degradation frequently related to huge-scale infrastructure initiatives.

The long-term sustainability of Hyperloop technology relies upon now not best on its instant environmental blessings however also on the way it scales and integrates into global transportation systems. As the sector transitions to purifier power sources and extra sustainable infrastructure, Hyperloop should play a vital function in reshaping the manner people and items move throughout the planet.

The potential for global carbon emissions reduction through full-size adoption of Hyperloop technology is gigantic.

If Hyperloop can correctly replace conventional transportation techniques, it could significantly reduce greenhouse fuel emissions from the transportation zone, one of the biggest individuals to worldwide warming. However, the environmental blessings will only be absolutely found out if the generation may be scaled up and integrated into current networks even as maintaining its energy performance and coffee-carbon design.

Hyperloop's capacity to lessen worldwide site visitors congestion additionally performs a role in its environmental impact. By supplying a quicker, more efficient mode of shipping, it is able to lessen the need for traditional road and rail delivery, alleviating some of the pressures on congested urban areas and decreasing the general environmental impact of transportation.

In the wider context, Hyperloop also can encourage improvements in other sectors, which include city planning, sustainable structure, and power systems. The classes found out from Hyperloop's environmental design should impact the improvement of other transportation technology and infrastructure projects, growing a greater sustainable global financial system.

The environmental impact of superior technologies like Hyperloop will in the long run depend upon how well they stability the advantages of innovation with the need to defend the planet's natural resources. Hyperloop's design principles—focused on electricity performance, sustainable substances, minimum waste, and ecosystem protection—position it as a capacity leader within the motion toward extra sustainable transportation systems. However, to absolutely comprehend its environmental ability, Hyperloop have to preserve to conform along improvements in renewable energy, useful resource control, and infrastructure development. By embracing sustainability at every level, Hyperloop can grow to be a transformative force in the combat in opposition to climate trade and a model for the environmentally-aware technologies of the destiny.

4.4. Sustainable Material Usage in Construction

The production of Hyperloop infrastructure represents a monumental engineering mission, demanding materials that no longer simplest meet stringent overall performance standards however also align with the principles of environmental sustainability. Sustainable material usage in Hyperloop production is crucial to minimizing the ecological footprint of the system at the same time as ensuring durability, protection, and cost-effectiveness. By integrating advanced, green substances and innovative constructing techniques, Hyperloop tasks purpose to set new requirements for responsible infrastructure development within the transportation quarter.

A essential issue of sustainable production for Hyperloop entails deciding on materials with low embodied carbon—the overall greenhouse gasoline emissions generated all through extraction, processing, manufacturing, and transportation. Traditional creation materials like conventional concrete and steel are strength-intensive to produce and make a contribution notably to international carbon emissions. To deal with this, Hyperloop engineers explore alternatives along with low-carbon concrete mixes that incorporate supplementary cementitious substances (SCMs) like fly ash or slag, which lessen the want for Portland cement and thereby decrease carbon output. Similarly, recycled metal and other metals with reduced manufacturing emissions are prioritized anyplace structural energy is critical.

Beyond carbon discount, fabric longevity and recyclability are essential considerations. Components utilized in Hyperloop infrastructure ought to resist severe mechanical stresses, environmental publicity, and ability seismic activity without common substitute or restore. Durable materials extend the lifecycle of the infrastructure, decreasing resource intake over time. Additionally, the layout contains factors which might be modular and recyclable, permitting materials to be recovered and reused at the cease of the gadget's carrier life, in addition lowering waste and environmental impact.

Innovative composites and bio-based substances also feature prominently in sustainable Hyperloop production. Advanced fiber-strengthened polymers provide excessive strength-to-weight ratios, corrosion resistance, and design flexibility, permitting lighter systems that require less raw cloth and strength to produce and delivery. Some initiatives look at the combination of bio-based totally binders or herbal fibers, which lessen reliance on fossil gas-derived products and decorate biodegradability.

Water performance at some point of production is any other critical factor. Techniques consisting of using recycled water in concrete manufacturing, rainwater harvesting on creation sites, and minimizing water-extensive methods assist preserve treasured freshwater resources. Managing runoff and stopping soil erosion via green infrastructure also align with sustainability desires.

Furthermore, sourcing substances domestically wherever viable reduces transportation emissions and helps regional economies. The proximity of suppliers can significantly decrease the carbon footprint related to logistics and foster network engagement with Hyperloop tasks.

Sustainable production practices are complemented by using smart design strategies geared toward decreasing cloth usage without compromising safety or overall performance. Optimization via pc modeling, prefabrication of components, and modular production techniques streamline the building system, minimize waste, and accelerate task timelines.

Sustainable fabric utilization in Hyperloop creation represents a holistic technique that balances environmental stewardship with the technical needs of a contemporary transportation system. By embracing low-carbon, durable, recyclable, and modern substances alongside green production practices, Hyperloop infrastructure exemplifies the potential for big-scale engineering projects to boost both technological progress and sustainability goals. This dedication not simplest allows mitigate the environmental impact of constructing the Hyperloop but additionally reinforces the generation's role as a pacesetter within the destiny of green transportation.

CHAPTER 5

Socioeconomic Impacts of Hyperloop

5.1. Impact on Living Spaces

The introduction of Hyperloop era is predicted to have profound consequences on human dwelling areas, reshaping the manner humans live, paintings, and engage with the environment round them. Hyperloop's capacity to significantly reduce travel instances among cities, regions, and even international locations will redefine how people and groups view their proximity to urban centers, doubtlessly altering the dynamics of residential and industrial spaces.

One of the maximum widespread affects of Hyperloop on dwelling areas might be the decentralization of city populations. Currently, large towns act because the valuable hubs of economic, cultural, and social lifestyles, attracting people due to activity opportunities, educational institutions, healthcare facilities, and leisure options. However, the time-consuming and regularly steeply-priced nature of transportation limits human beings's potential to live in greater rural or suburban regions while nevertheless preserving get right of entry to to urban advantages. Hyperloop's promise of near-on the spot tour will lessen those barriers, permitting people to stay in extra spacious, less expensive regions far from crowded city facilities without sacrificing get admission to to work, commerce, and offerings.

For instance, individuals may want to pick out to stay in quieter suburban neighborhoods or maybe in smaller towns, as Hyperloop will permit them to go back and forth effortlessly to main towns for paintings or enjoyment. This shift may want to ease the pressures of urbanization, alleviating overcrowding in megacities and mitigating problems inclusive of housing shortages, excessive dwelling prices, and environmental degradation. Instead of feeling compelled to transport to a town for higher task potentialities or social opportunities, people will have the liberty to choose a living region that suits their lifestyle, whether it's close to nature, greater inexpensive housing, or surely a much less demanding surroundings.

Hyperloop's efficiency may also bring a rethinking of the concept of "home" and how a long way people are willing to tour for work or leisure. With travel instances substantially reduced, human beings ought to live in addition faraway from their place of work or preferred destinations, correctly creating greater accessible groups and economic regions. Hyperloop can also flip long commutes right into a aspect of the beyond, allowing for a extra various range of residential regions to flourish as human beings are no longer tethered to dwelling near their jobs. This should cause a extra flippantly distributed populace and a more balanced use of land, assisting to counter urban sprawl and maintain herbal environments.

The adjustments in dwelling spaces will no longer most effective be bodily however also social. With the expansion of on hand areas via Hyperloop, people might broaden more potent local identities and stronger connections with remote communities, helping to reduce the isolation that frequently occurs in far off regions. As towns end up more interconnected, the opportunities for fostering move-cultural interactions and collaborations boom. For instance, human beings dwelling in small towns ought to extra effortlessly attend events, exhibitions, and conferences in foremost towns or interact with specialists from around the arena. Similarly, specialists ought to relocate to quieter, extra peaceful regions without demanding approximately losing get right of entry to to profession possibilities or professional networks.

Additionally, belongings values in regions close to Hyperloop stations are in all likelihood to increase as the ease of connectivity turns into a premium selling factor. Areas with access to Hyperloop will in all likelihood entice new investments and concrete improvement, growing a combination of residential, business, and combined-use areas that cater to the brand new wishes of a mobile, interconnected society. Real estate builders may be keen to build new houses, offices, and amusement venues near Hyperloop stations to take gain of this accelerated connectivity. This may want to spur the boom of vibrant, self-maintaining communities round those hubs, blending comfort with livability.

However, these changes may even come with ability demanding situations. The speedy improvement of regions round Hyperloop stations may additionally cause improved call for for land, using up prices and probably making it harder for lower-earnings individuals to find low priced housing in high locations. As extra humans flock to these regions, governments and nearby authorities will want to manipulate urban making plans and infrastructure improvement carefully to save you gentrification and make sure that those new hubs remain reachable to a diverse populace.

Moreover, whilst the decentralization of populations can also reduce the pressures on city areas, it is able to also strain rural or suburban regions that might not have the necessary infrastructure to guide a fast inflow of human beings. Local governments will want to prepare for capability populace booms, upgrading housing, healthcare, colleges, and utilities to house the growing populace. This may want to contain massive investment in infrastructure to ensure that newly evolved areas are not simplest handy however also sustainable in the long run.

Hyperloop's impact on residing spaces will be transformative, imparting people greater alternatives concerning wherein they live and the way they interact with the world. By decreasing the limitations of tour time and distance, it will permit a brand new wave of city planning that emphasizes mobility, connectivity, and high-quality of lifestyles.

While challenges associated with infrastructure, housing, and economic inequality may additionally get up, the general impact of Hyperloop might be a more balanced and dynamic approach to urban improvement, growing thriving, interconnected groups that sell growth, inclusivity, and sustainability.

5.2. Workforce and Job Opportunities: New Horizons

The implementation of Hyperloop technology is poised to generate sizable shifts in the global hard work marketplace and create new opportunities across various sectors. By revolutionizing transportation and enabling ultra-speedy journey among towns and areas, Hyperloop will no longer most effective influence how humans pass however will even remodel industries, economies, and the manner human beings work. From new process classes to the emergence of novel industries, Hyperloop could have a profound impact on the personnel and activity opportunities in each direct and indirect ways.

One of the number one results of Hyperloop could be the creation of completely new activity possibilities in studies, engineering, production, and operational fields. The design, development, and upkeep of Hyperloop structures would require a pretty professional staff in more than one disciplines. Engineers specializing in transportation systems, electromagnetic generation, vacuum technologies, and structural design will be in excessive call for, as these are important regions to ensuring the a hit implementation of the gadget. The development of Hyperloop may even necessitate improvements in energy structures, protection mechanisms, and automation technology, generating further task opportunities in areas like strength production, cybersecurity, and robotics.

In addition to the technological personnel needed to create and keep Hyperloop infrastructure, there could be sizable demand for workers in assist industries. The production of Hyperloop stations, terminals, and networks will require a wide variety of employees, from architects and urban planners to production employees and facility managers. The operations of Hyperloop systems themselves, along with ticketing, scheduling, customer support, and everyday control, will also cause the introduction of plenty of provider-associated jobs. As Hyperloop becomes operational and the technology scales, the call for for fairly professional employees in logistics, statistics evaluation, and network management will develop exponentially.

Hyperloop's potential to lessen travel time throughout substantial distances may also have a profound effect on nearby labor markets. Remote or rural areas, that have historically struggled to attract companies because of their geographic isolation, will be capable of compete for skills and funding.

High-velocity connections will allow workers to stay some distance from their employers at the same time as still commuting to work in a fragment of the time it takes today. As a result, agencies in important urban centers may additionally locate it less difficult to recruit skills from a broader geographical pool, leading to extra possibilities for employees in formerly underserved regions. This shift will now not simplest advantage the skills pool but will even support the growth of nearby economies as industries in those regions gain get right of entry to to a bigger personnel.

Additionally, industries related to tourism, amusement, and entertainment will experience full-size increase due to Hyperloop's ability to connect remote regions quite simply. As tour becomes quicker and extra on hand, human beings may have more possibilities to visit neighboring cities, attend conferences or activities, and engage in leisure activities without the burdens of lengthy travel times. This ease of travel will stimulate demand for workers in hospitality, retail, and tourism, main to process advent in industries that depend on tourism and leisure sports. The increased movement of human beings and goods will further improve activity possibilities in distribution, supply chain control, and services assisting these sectors.

Beyond unique industries, Hyperloop's broader financial effect will possibly lead to the development of absolutely new sectors. Hyperloop may want to pave the way for new kinds of trade that depend upon the fast motion of goods and offerings among remote places. The reduction in transportation time and charges could create extra efficient supply chains, prompting corporations to undertake new logistics fashions that contain quicker and greater dynamic inventory control. This should bring about job creation in fields like logistics, warehousing, and stock control, in addition to in emerging sectors along with virtual reality buying and stay-streamed activities, where geographical boundaries emerge as less of a constraint.

The development of Hyperloop may even have implications for the gig financial system, which has seen rapid increase in current years. As the capacity to journey quickly among towns becomes a reality, people may increasingly more choose freelance or agreement work, understanding that they can without problems tour to diverse places to satisfy with clients or employers. This could result in a rise in far off working opportunities, allowing employees to provide their offerings to businesses across the globe at the same time as retaining a bendy lifestyle. Hyperloop may additionally in the long run help the idea of a "worldwide body of workers," where area is now not a constraint for activity opportunities. This dynamic would foster new fashions of collaboration and innovation, with workers being capable of perform throughout borders with little to no drawback.

However, the huge adoption of Hyperloop technology also brings challenges to the prevailing group of workers. As industries are reshaped and transportation becomes quicker and extra efficient, a few conventional process roles can be rendered obsolete or face extensive disruption. For example, jobs in lengthy-distance transportation, such as those in trucking or conventional rail systems, will be negatively impacted with the aid of the shift toward quicker and greater efficient tour. There can also be a want for retraining applications to ensure that people in conventional sectors are ready with the skills vital to thrive inside the new financial system. Governments, educational establishments, and companies will want to collaborate to develop reskilling tasks that prepare the workforce for the roles of the following day.

Moreover, the upward thrust of automation in Hyperloop systems, including self-using pods, computerized ticketing, and AI-pushed preservation, might also lead to personnel displacement in some areas. The automation of delivery and associated industries ought to reduce the variety of jobs in positive sectors, despite the fact that it can also lead to task creation in fields which include AI improvement, programming, and system upkeep. Balancing automation with employment opportunities might be a essential venture for policymakers and enterprise leaders for you to make sure a smooth transition for workers whose jobs may be tormented by these adjustments.

Hyperloop technology has the ability to create a extensive variety of job opportunities across numerous sectors, from engineering and generation to hospitality, logistics, and past. By facilitating faster, extra green travel, it'll open up new avenues for personnel mobility, allowing workers to access job opportunities across broader geographic areas. However, these modifications will require cautious planning and consideration to make certain that workers are equipped with the skills had to be triumphant within the evolving exertions marketplace. The Hyperloop revolution will undoubtedly redefine the manner humans paintings, creating exciting new opportunities whilst also imparting challenges on the way to require proactive edition.

5.3. Economic Growth and Global Transformation

The introduction of Hyperloop generation holds the potential to ignite tremendous economic boom and catalyze a profound transformation in international economies. By drastically decreasing journey instances among towns and international locations, Hyperloop will foster greater green alternate, boost up the movement of goods and offerings, and make a contribution to the introduction of recent industries. This innovation is poised to reshape global financial landscapes, developing a more interconnected international wherein borders are much less of an impediment, and markets are extra fluid.

One of the number one ways in which Hyperloop will make contributions to monetary growth is through the facilitation of fast and value-effective transportation. By imparting an efficient opportunity to present day sorts of long-distance journey, along with trains, airplanes, and road delivery, Hyperloop can lessen logistical prices for businesses and enhance the performance of deliver chains. With goods and services shifting extra fast and reliably, industries that rely upon timely shipping will see their operational efficiency improve, allowing corporations to amplify into new markets with greater ease. This may be especially beneficial for industries like manufacturing, retail, and agriculture, wherein transportation expenses are a considerable part of the overall production value structure.

As Hyperloop quickens the movement of people and goods, it's going to open up new financial opportunities for regions formerly remote with the aid of distance. Areas that are far from main financial hubs can become greater integrated into international trade networks, imparting them with get right of entry to to larger markets and fostering monetary improvement. For example, cities and towns that have been as soon as too far off to attract investment or a skilled hard work pressure may want to gain from Hyperloop's ability to drastically shorten journey instances. The potential to journey speedy to essential metropolitan areas will allow businesses in those regions to draw skills and funding, that may cause new financial increase centers out of doors traditional city powerhouses. This democratization of get right of entry to will assist reduce nearby financial disparities and create a greater balanced global economic system.

In addition to facilitating trade, Hyperloop will stimulate innovation by using permitting quicker conversation and collaboration between corporations and studies establishments. The ability to easily travel to key hubs for medical and technological studies, commercial enterprise conferences, and meetings will facilitate cross-border collaboration, permitting international partnerships to flourish. This elevated alternate of thoughts, technology, and know-how will gas innovation across diverse industries, inclusive of healthcare, energy, and environmental technology. As industries grow to be greater interconnected, the price of technological development will probable boost up, further propelling international financial boom.

Moreover, the creation of Hyperloop infrastructure itself can have a massive monetary effect. The development of Hyperloop structures would require good sized investments in studies and improvement, production, and upkeep. This will result in activity advent in industries which includes construction, engineering, task management, and manufacturing, growing vast brief-time period monetary interest. Over the long time, the operation and preservation of Hyperloop structures will aid a extensive variety of industries, from transportation and logistics to customer service and administrative functions. The demand for professional employees in regions which includes electromagnetics, systems engineering, and automation can even contribute to the wider economy, making sure that information-in depth sectors thrive along extra conventional industries.

Furthermore, Hyperloop generation can even create new enterprise fashions and open up absolutely new industries. The capability to journey speedy and effectively will transform the tourism and amusement sectors by making formerly remote locations extra on hand. Cities that have been as soon as taken into consideration too faraway for tourism may be able to appeal to visitors from all over the international, stimulating neighborhood economies. The discount in journey time will make it feasible for humans to go to a couple of places in a single day, starting the door to new business ventures in areas which includes hospitality, meals services, and enjoyment. New styles of tourism, together with "hyper-tourism," wherein humans take short journeys to go to multiple towns or nations, will emerge, leading to increased demand for transportation offerings and infrastructure, in addition to new financial possibilities for those working in the tourism enterprise.

In addition to tourism, industries tied to global connectivity, which include finance and actual property, will even see transformative modifications. As tour between cities becomes faster, specialists in sectors like banking, insurance, and consultancy can be capable of enlarge their geographical attain. High-velocity connections will enable them to preserve face-to-face meetings with customers in multiple cities in a single day, driving enterprise increase and fostering stronger monetary ties among areas. Likewise, the real estate market will be tormented by the increased accessibility of distant regions. Urban sprawl, which has historically been driven by the look for inexpensive land and housing alternatives at the outskirts of important towns, could be reversed as Hyperloop makes it feasible to live similarly away from urban facilities even as nonetheless commuting quick and effortlessly. This shift in actual estate patterns may want to cause new financial hubs emerging in formerly underdeveloped regions.

Hyperloop's effect on the worldwide economic system extends beyond individual industries to broader shifts in the manner economies operate. The technology will facilitate a greater integrated, global economic system via putting off the traditional obstacles posed by way of distance and time. The movement of humans, goods, and offerings becomes more seamless, reducing friction in global exchange and opening up markets that were once out of reach for organizations in smaller or greater isolated areas. This will inspire competition, foster innovation, and offer purchasers with a greater variety of products and offerings at more aggressive fees, all of that allows you to make contributions to global economic increase.

However, those capability benefits can even bring about challenges. The improved financial integration enabled by means of Hyperloop should exacerbate present inequalities, specifically between regions and international locations which have get right of entry to to Hyperloop systems and those that don't. While some regions will see giant monetary boom because of stepped forward connectivity, others may additionally warfare to capture up, growing an opening among the haves and feature-nots within the global economic system. Ensuring that the blessings of Hyperloop are lightly disbursed will require cautious planning and investment in infrastructure, technology, and schooling to ensure that each one areas are capable of take advantage of the brand new opportunities created with the aid of the gadget.

Additionally, the implementation of Hyperloop generation will require significant monetary funding and international cooperation, which might also present challenges in phrases of securing funding and navigating political landscapes. Countries with current superior transportation structures can be extra willing to undertake Hyperloop generation, while those with much less evolved infrastructures might also face more obstacles to entry. Therefore, policymakers will want to cautiously keep in mind a way to finance Hyperloop tasks and ensure that they advantage each developed and developing areas.

Hyperloop technology has the capacity to seriously increase global monetary increase by transforming industries, increasing performance, and opening up new markets. By lowering transportation charges, permitting faster motion of products and services, and fostering innovation, Hyperloop may want to fundamentally reshape the way the global economy features. As the technology develops and expands, it's going to create new possibilities for groups, governments, and individuals alike. However, ensuring that the blessings of Hyperloop are disbursed equitably and addressing the challenges of financing and political cooperation could be critical to ensuring its lengthy-time period fulfillment in reworking the worldwide economic system.

5.4. Addressing Economic Inequalities

The deployment of Hyperloop generation holds gigantic promise for remodeling worldwide transportation, but it also raises vital questions about monetary inequality. While the gadget offers quicker, greater green, and potentially extra cheap tour, its blessings ought to be allotted equitably to avoid exacerbating present socioeconomic divides. Addressing economic inequalities within the context of Hyperloop implementation calls for deliberate strategies that ensure accessibility, inclusivity, and fair possibility for all segments of society.

At the forefront of those concerns is the issue of access. Historically, major transportation advancements have every now and then desired wealthier populations or city centers, leaving marginalized or rural groups underserved. Hyperloop tasks, if not carefully planned, chance repeating this pattern by normally connecting prosperous towns or regions wherein investment yields higher returns. To counter this, policymakers and planners should prioritize inclusive direction planning that links economically deprived areas to larger financial hubs, thereby opening pathways for employment, training, and services that could uplift nearby populations.

Affordability is some other vital element. The high initial expenses of Hyperloop infrastructure and operations can also translate into premium ticket fees which are out of reach for low-earnings individuals. To mitigate this, public subsidies, tiered pricing fashions, or government partnerships may be hired to keep fare systems which are accessible to various profits organizations. Ensuring equitable pricing enables prevent transportation deserts and helps social mobility with the aid of allowing broader segments of the populace to gain from rapid transit.

Job introduction linked to Hyperloop construction and operation additionally has the capacity to deal with economic inequalities. Large-scale infrastructure projects regularly stimulate neighborhood economies by using generating employment opportunities. Emphasizing body of workers improvement applications that teach and employ individuals from underrepresented or disadvantaged communities can help bridge income gaps. Furthermore, the emergence of recent industries and offerings round Hyperloop networks can foster entrepreneurial interest and financial diversification in areas previously left behind.

However, the economic ripple effects of Hyperloop may additionally pose demanding situations. Rapid connectivity can increase belongings values and residing charges in newly available areas, doubtlessly displacing decrease-income residents thru gentrification. To control these unintentional results, included urban making plans and housing policies need to be implemented in tandem with Hyperloop development to preserve lower priced housing and defend vulnerable communities.

Moreover, equitable get admission to to Hyperloop should be complemented through complementary investments in local infrastructure along with public transit, roads, and digital connectivity. Without these, the full advantages of Hyperloop connectivity might also fail to reach marginalized populations who face limitations within the "last mile" of journey or lack resources to capitalize on new opportunities.

Finally, worldwide cooperation and inclusive governance fashions are essential to make sure that the economic blessings of Hyperloop generation do not pay attention totally within wealthy international locations or agencies. International standards, expertise sharing, and honest funding practices can assist democratize get admission to to Hyperloop innovation, fostering a extra balanced international financial panorama.

Addressing monetary inequalities within the technology of Hyperloop transportation calls for a multifaceted approach that combines inclusive making plans, less costly pricing, workforce empowerment, and defensive social rules. By proactively confronting these demanding situations, Hyperloop can come to be not best a image of technological progress however additionally a catalyst for more social fairness and monetary justice international.

CHAPTER 6

Hyperloop and Other Transportation Technologies

6.1. Comparison with Trains, Cars, and Airplanes

The advent of Hyperloop generation guarantees to revolutionize transportation through offering a faster, extra green alternative to conventional land and air travel. To completely recognize the importance of Hyperloop inside the context of current transportation, it's far essential to compare it with present modes of journey: trains, cars, and airplanes. Each of those transportation technology has performed a pivotal function in shaping human mobility, yet they every have inherent boundaries that Hyperloop targets to triumph over.

Trains have lengthy been a cornerstone of land-based transportation, in particular for mass transit over long distances. They are regarded for his or her capability to transport massive numbers of passengers efficaciously and for being a enormously electricity-green mode of travel. However, conventional rail structures face numerous challenges that restrict their capability and pace.

First, educate tour is restrained via the prevailing rail infrastructure, that is regularly previous or incompatible with more moderen excessive-speed technology. High-speed trains, such as Japan's Shinkansen and France's TGV, can attain speeds upwards of 300 km/h (186 mph), however their overall performance continues to be constrained through friction between the tracks and wheels, in addition to the want for frequent stops and slowdowns for safety and operational motives. Furthermore, the development and upkeep of excessive-velocity rail networks may be prohibitively expensive, specially in areas with mountainous terrain or densely populated urban areas.

In assessment, Hyperloop technology operates in a vacuum tube, lowering the effect of friction and air resistance. This lets in Hyperloop pods to attain speeds a ways extra than those of traditional trains. While the quickest trains on the market can gain speeds of around 300 km/h, Hyperloop has the ability to reach speeds in excess of 1,000 km/h (620 mph). This dramatic increase in speed, coupled with the lack of direct interaction with the track infrastructure, enables Hyperloop to provide extensively quicker journey times, specifically over long distances.

Additionally, Hyperloop's reduced reliance on bodily rail tracks approach that it can be deployed extra effortlessly in areas where conventional rail networks would be costly or logistically difficult to implement, along with faraway places or areas with excessive populace densities.

Cars are possibly the maximum extensively used shape of transportation round the arena. They offer unheard of freedom, allowing individuals to tour at their very own tempo, pick out their very own routes, and access definitely any location on land. However, the widespread use of vehicles comes with vast drawbacks.

For one, automobiles are closely depending on street infrastructure, which in lots of cases is already overcrowded, particularly in city regions. Traffic congestion, lengthy go back and forth instances, and common injuries are all not unusual problems associated with automobile tour. Additionally, vehicles contribute appreciably to environmental pollution, in particular in phrases of carbon emissions, and are a main contributor to climate alternate.

From a safety angle, cars are problem to street dangers, injuries, and human blunders, that could bring about accidents or fatalities. Even although advancements in vehicle protection technology and the development of autonomous cars are enhancing the scenario, road journey remains one of the riskiest styles of transportation.

Hyperloop, by contrast, promises a much more secure and more efficient alternative. The vacuum tube gadget gets rid of outside variables including climate, street conditions, and accidents, appreciably reducing the likelihood of delays or crashes. Furthermore, because the pods are guided alongside a predefined path in a managed surroundings, the risks related to human mistakes are minimized. The safety features of Hyperloop, including automated structures and redundancies, make it a doubtlessly a ways more secure choice as compared to riding a automobile on public roads.

Additionally, Hyperloop may want to lessen the need for motors in city regions, as it'd provide a faster, extra convenient mode of journey. This should alleviate traffic congestion, reduce air pollution, and result in a extra sustainable form of city mobility. By integrating Hyperloop into current transportation networks, people should seamlessly transition from vehicle tour to high-speed, efficient Hyperloop structures, improving the overall performance of world mobility.

Airplanes have long been the gold popular for long-distance journey, presenting unrivaled speeds compared to any land-based totally transportation option. Commercial airliners can journey at speeds of over 900 km/h (560 mph), protecting sizable distances in a fraction of the time it'd take a educate or vehicle. However, the advantages of air journey come with numerous large challenges.

One of the number one drawbacks of air tour is its reliance on airports, which can be normally placed out of doors urban facilities and require giant time for passengers to reach. Airports themselves also are notorious for lengthy wait instances, safety assessments, delays, and baggage coping with. These logistical challenges can make air travel time-ingesting, specially whilst considering the time spent getting to and from airports, going through security, and waiting for flights.

Moreover, whilst air travel is speedy, it isn't always always the most efficient, especially when thinking about the environmental impact. Airplanes are considerable contributors to carbon emissions, and the aviation industry faces growing pressure to reduce its environmental footprint. While some technological advancements, inclusive of electric planes and biofuels, show promise, those answers are nevertheless within the early tiers of improvement.

Hyperloop gives numerous blessings over airplanes, especially for short to medium distances. While airplanes are most effective for lengthy-haul tour, Hyperloop is higher proper for journeys of below 1,000 km, where the velocity and convenience of air journey are much less said. Hyperloop gets rid of the need for airport infrastructure, supplying a unbroken, direct connection between cities or urban hubs without the delays and trouble of airport tactics.

Additionally, Hyperloop guarantees a far lower environmental impact than airplanes. As a fully electric machine, it may be powered through renewable power resources, decreasing its carbon footprint drastically compared to the aviation enterprise. Hyperloop also minimizes energy consumption through its vacuum tube and magnetic propulsion systems, making it a extra electricity-green mode of transportation than planes.

While trains, motors, and airplanes have every performed a vital role in shaping modern transportation networks, Hyperloop affords a compelling alternative that addresses many of the inefficiencies, protection concerns, and environmental challenges associated with conventional structures. By combining the speed of air travel with the performance of trains and the safety of cars, Hyperloop represents a paradigm shift in how we consider shifting humans and goods across sizable distances.

Although the giant adoption of Hyperloop is still inside the early stages, its potential to revolutionize transportation is vast. As technology continues to conform and the feasibility of Hyperloop will become greater obvious, it's miles probably to play a pivotal position in the future of mobility, presenting a quicker, safer, and extra sustainable alternative to the modes of transportation we rely on today.

6.2. Hyperloop's Speed and Safety Advantages

Hyperloop technology stands out now not handiest for its capability to redefine the future of transportation however also for the giant advantages it offers in phrases of pace and protection. These factors are vital inside the improvement and adoption of any new mode of journey, and Hyperloop addresses the inherent limitations of conventional shipping structures with progressive answers.

One of the most compelling capabilities of Hyperloop is its exceptional pace. Hyperloop's design permits it to potentially exceed the speeds of present day modes of transportation, making it a sport-changer for intercity or even regional travel.

Hyperloop pods, that are designed to tour in a near-vacuum surroundings, face appreciably less air resistance than conventional trains or automobiles. Traditional transportation systems are hindered by way of the friction among wheels and rails, or tires and street surfaces, which limits their most pace. By reducing air resistance to a minimal and doing away with physical friction, Hyperloop pods can theoretically attain speeds in extra of 1,000 km/h (620 mph), almost three times faster than excessive-pace trains and much quicker than maximum business airplanes for shorter distances.

The vacuum tube device in which the pods travel basically creates a frictionless surroundings, allowing the pods to flow at high speeds with minimum power input. With much less energy required to conquer resistance, Hyperloop isn't always simplest faster however additionally doubtlessly greater electricity-efficient than conventional methods of transportation.

This velocity advantage has some distance-accomplishing implications. Hyperloop can remodel the concept of tour among major cities, appreciably decreasing the time it takes to go back and forth between them. For example, a journey that currently takes numerous hours through car, train, or plane could be reduced to a count number of minutes. In the case of distances below 1,000 km, Hyperloop could end up the most efficient way to travel, outperforming conventional modes of transportation.

Moreover, Hyperloop's velocity does no longer come on the value of comfort. The whole machine is designed for easy, uninterrupted travel. Unlike airplanes, which require take a look at-in, safety screenings, and lengthy boarding strategies, Hyperloop passengers can expect speedy and efficient travel, with minimal time spent at stations.

Safety is a important issue of any transportation gadget, and while conventional modes of transport consisting of vehicles, trains, and airplanes have well-hooked up safety protocols, Hyperloop promises to set a brand new benchmark for protection in travel.

Hyperloop operates in a controlled vacuum tube device that removes most of the safety risks associated with traditional transportation. In conventional systems, vehicles are challenge to external variables such as weather situations, road excellent, and traffic, all of which could cause accidents. Hyperloop, however, isn't stricken by weather situations, because the enclosed tube shields the pods from external environmental factors. This means that passengers can travel in any climate—

rain, snow, or extreme warmness—with out the hazard of delays or injuries caused by unpredictable situations.

Safety features within Hyperloop also are enhanced by using using automated manipulate structures. These structures are designed to screen the pods and infrastructure in real time, ensuring that the device operates smoothly and thoroughly. In the event of an problem or malfunction, automated backups are in place to prevent injuries, similar to the fail-safe mechanisms seen in modern-day aviation.

The use of sensors and AI-powered systems to discover capability issues along with system screw ups or emergencies lets in the system to reply instantly. Additionally, Hyperloop pods are designed to be modular, which means that in the event of a malfunction, the gadget can isolate and comprise the issue, ensuring that different pods at the network aren't affected. This disbursed method minimizes the chance of giant disruption and enhances the overall protection of the device.

One of the most important demanding situations for safety in transportation is ensuring that there are good enough emergency protocols in location. While airplanes, trains, and vehicles all have nicely-set up safety measures, the enclosed environment of the Hyperloop provides new demanding situations. However, designers of the Hyperloop system have evolved complete emergency protocols to address those demanding situations. Hyperloop stations could be prepared with advanced emergency evacuation methods, permitting passengers to exit the system properly in the not going event of an emergency.

The pods themselves are also designed to make sure the protection of passengers in severe situations. In the occasion of a mechanical failure or breach in the tube, emergency air strain structures might have interaction to defend passengers from ability harm. The pods will also have onboard existence support structures, ensuring that passengers remain secure and snug even in the case of unexpected disruptions.

A enormous thing in transportation injuries—especially in aviation and road journey—is human errors. Hyperloop's automatic systems lessen the want for human intervention, as a consequence minimizing the risks associated with operator errors. While human mistakes nonetheless performs a position in the design and maintenance of the infrastructure, the structures within Hyperloop are constructed to self-adjust and modify to adjustments or malfunctions in actual time.

Furthermore, the Hyperloop community operates below strict protocols, which means that best in particular skilled employees could be worried inside the operation and upkeep of the device. This is just like the stringent rules inside the aviation enterprise, in which pilots and team go through in depth training and certification.

While the theoretical blessings of Hyperloop in terms of pace and safety are spectacular, its sensible implementation remains in progress. Prototypes and take a look at tracks are being evolved round the sector, with groups like Virgin Hyperloop and Elon Musk's The Boring Company main the price. In the approaching years, in addition improvement, checking out, and refinement may be necessary to make sure that Hyperloop can operate at its maximum ability.

Despite these challenges, the future of Hyperloop as a fast, safe, and green mode of transportation looks promising. As advancements in era preserve and actual-international trying out progresses, Hyperloop could revolutionize tour, presenting a level of pace and protection that surpasses any transportation gadget in operation these days.

Hyperloop gives an exciting new frontier in transportation, with its pace and safety benefits positioning it as a capability recreation-changer. The gadget's capacity to gain speeds nicely above current land and air tour, coupled with its superior safety mechanisms, makes it an exceptionally appealing alternative for the future of mobility. While there are still hurdles to overcome in terms of generation, infrastructure, and implementation, the ability advantages of Hyperloop in phrases of velocity and protection are plain, and it's far probably to play a sizable role in shaping the destiny of journey.

6.3. The Future of Traditional Transportation Systems

As progressive technology which include Hyperloop maintain to boost, they improve vital questions about the future of traditional transportation structures. While Hyperloop guarantees a revolution in high-pace journey, it does no longer mean the on the spot obsolescence of trains, cars, or airplanes. Rather, the destiny of traditional transportation systems lies in how they adapt to the changing landscape of mobility, combine with new technology, and maintain to serve the diverse needs of global journey.

Trains have lengthy been a staple of global transportation, providing a reliable, green, and environmentally friendly method of travel over land. The destiny of rail delivery lies within the persisted improvement of excessive-velocity trains and their integration with futuristic structures like Hyperloop.

The fulfillment of high-pace rail structures in countries inclusive of Japan, France, and China has established that trains may be an excellent alternative to air tour for quick to medium distances. These trains, which reach speeds up to 300 km/h (186 mph), have proven their potential to seriously lessen journey instances among important towns, presenting a extraordinarily aggressive opportunity to traditional air tour.

However, excessive-velocity rail faces limitations, specially in phrases of infrastructure expenses and the time it takes to increase new structures. As Hyperloop becomes more viable, there may be a shift in the direction of integrating rail and Hyperloop structures to create hybrid transportation networks. For example, Hyperloop should serve as the primary high-pace spine between main cities, at the same time as excessive-speed trains continue to offer efficient neighborhood connections and offerings to areas that Hyperloop can not attain.

In the future, the rail enterprise may also evolve to encompass self sustaining trains, which might enhance safety and operational performance. Automated systems may want to reduce human blunders, optimize scheduling, and offer passengers a more seamless and comfortable experience. The mixture of excessive-velocity trains and Hyperloop could bring about an advanced, interconnected transportation machine that maximizes the strengths of each technology.

Cars have revolutionized private mobility, and they may continue to be a giant a part of the transportation panorama for the foreseeable destiny. However, the destiny of road travel will probable go through an intensive transformation due to improvements in self sufficient automobile (AV) technology, electrification, and integration with smart infrastructure.

Autonomous cars, already being examined via organizations inclusive of Tesla, Waymo, and others, represent a fundamental shift in how humans will journey by using vehicle. These self-riding automobiles have the capacity to significantly lessen visitors injuries, enhance gas efficiency, and make commuting more handy by means of putting off the need for human drivers. AVs may be capable of speak with each different and with smart infrastructure to optimize visitors glide, reduce congestion, and limit environmental effect.

In addition to self sufficient driving, the transition to electric cars (EVs) is already underway. With improvements in battery generation, EVs have become greater low-priced, green, and capable of lengthy-variety tour. This shift to electric powered vehicles aligns with worldwide efforts to reduce carbon emissions and combat weather alternate. As EVs emerge as the norm, the conventional fuel-powered car will steadily segment out, ushering in a new technology of cleaner, quieter, and extra efficient transportation.

The creation of Hyperloop does no longer signal the give up of cars, but as an alternative a shift within the kinds of journey motors are maximum proper for. Hyperloop will revolutionize long-distance travel, but for quick journeys and local commuting, self sufficient electric powered automobiles will play a key role. These cars may be able to seamlessly combine with Hyperloop structures, allowing passengers to journey quick from their houses to Hyperloop stations and vice versa.

Aviation has long been the dominant mode of delivery for long-distance journey. Despite the improvements of Hyperloop, airplanes will preserve to play a vital position in global transportation, specially for worldwide tour and locations which are a ways beyond the attain of land-based totally transportation systems.

However, the destiny of aviation will appearance exclusive as new technologies which includes electric powered and hybrid-electric powered plane are developed. Companies like Boeing and Airbus are already making an investment in sustainable aviation technology, which aim to lessen the environmental impact of air travel. Electric planes, able to flying short to medium distances with zero emissions, are expected to enter industrial carrier in the next few decades.

While Hyperloop can offer a sizeable gain for home and nearby tour, airplanes will nonetheless be important for global flights and tour to remote regions. The future of aviation will contain combining sustainable practices with the speed and efficiency that contemporary air travel offers. Airplanes will probable continue to conform, with an increasing attention on minimizing their carbon footprint and enhancing gasoline efficiency.

One potential manner that Hyperloop and aviation structures can supplement each different is through using "ultimate-mile" answers. Hyperloop could shipping passengers among principal city hubs, and from there, airplanes may want to take over for international travel, creating a seamless community for travelers.

The future of traditional public transportation will also be motivated through improvements in Hyperloop generation. In most important city centers, the role of buses, subways, and trams will evolve as these systems emerge as more integrated with Hyperloop networks.

In the approaching years, many cities will adopt "clever town" era, which leverages information, automation, and advanced connectivity to optimize the drift of human beings and items. Public transportation will increasingly depend on computerized structures and dynamic routing to fulfill the changing needs of the population. Hyperloop stations may want to function important hubs that join seamlessly with neighborhood public transport systems, permitting passengers to transition smoothly from one mode of journey to every other.

In the destiny, cities may additionally adopt transportation structures that combine multiple modes of journey right into a single, unified revel in. For example, a traveler could board a Hyperloop pod, travel among towns at ultra-high speeds, after which take a driverless car or a nearby transit bus to reach their final destination.

While Hyperloop guarantees to revolutionize excessive-velocity journey, conventional transportation systems will keep to conform and adapt. Trains, cars, and airplanes are far from obsolete; alternatively, they'll coexist with Hyperloop as part of a complete transportation community.

The destiny of conventional transportation structures is one in every of integration and innovation. Advances in self sufficient driving, electric powered vehicles, and sustainable aviation will complement the excessive-speed, low-resistance journey presented via Hyperloop. Rather than replacing existing structures, Hyperloop will paintings in tandem with them to create a seamless and efficient international transportation network.

Ultimately, the destiny of transportation will not be described by one era on my own however by the synergy among vintage and new, with each device playing a unique position in assembly the numerous needs of current vacationers.

6.4. Integration with Existing Transport Networks

The a hit implementation of Hyperloop generation relies upon closely on its seamless integration with existing transportation networks. As a modern mode of transit designed to function at unprecedented speeds, Hyperloop can't function in isolation if it ambitions to function a realistic and on hand mobility answer. Instead, it ought to be thoughtfully related with traditional infrastructure such as nearby public transit structures, railways, road networks, and airports to create a comprehensive, multimodal transportation environment that maximizes convenience and efficiency for users.

One of the key demanding situations in integrating Hyperloop with current networks is ensuring clean transitions among special modes of travel. Passengers normally rely upon a mixture of transportation kinds to finish their journeys — from local buses and subways to regional trains and taxis. Hyperloop stations have to therefore be strategically placed and designed to facilitate clean transfers, minimizing on foot distances, wait times, and logistical complexities. Integrated ticketing systems and actual-time scheduling coordination throughout one of a kind modes enhance this connectivity, allowing tourists to plot their trips effortlessly and enjoy a cohesive journey revel in.

Moreover, Hyperloop's infrastructure, frequently improved or tunneled to hold its vacuum surroundings, gives precise opportunities and constraints for integration. Elevated Hyperloop strains may be constructed above current highways or rail corridors, lowering land acquisition challenges and environmental disruption. Conversely, Hyperloop hubs need to attach efficaciously with floor-level transit, requiring well-designed interchanges, parking facilities, and pedestrian get entry to. Urban planners and engineers ought to collaborate carefully to harmonize those bodily interfaces, balancing spatial constraints and person wishes.

From an operational perspective, information sharing and conversation between Hyperloop control systems and traditional transportation control facilities are essential. Synchronizing schedules and coping with passenger flows facilitates save you bottlenecks and optimizes network-huge efficiency. Additionally, integrating Hyperloop's automated manage technology with existing safety and emergency protocols ensures that multimodal networks can reply speedy and cohesively to incidents, maintaining excessive requirements of safety and reliability.

Financially, integration opens pathways for collaborative investment fashions related to public agencies, personal businesses, and worldwide stakeholders. Funding coordinated infrastructure improvements and shared operational structures reduces duplication of resources and leverages the strengths of diverse companions. It additionally fosters innovation via shared technology and satisfactory practices, accelerating the development of an interconnected mobility destiny.

Finally, integrating Hyperloop with present transportation networks has broader social and environmental implications. By connecting fast, long-distance tour with reachable nearby transit, it encourages the use of public transportation over private vehicles, decreasing site visitors congestion, pollution, and concrete sprawl. This synergy supports sustainable city increase and complements the satisfactory of life for groups.

The integration of Hyperloop era with present day transport systems is important for knowing its complete ability.

Thoughtful making plans, infrastructure design, technological coordination, and collaborative investment are necessary to create a unified, green, and consumer-friendly mobility community. Through those efforts, Hyperloop can turn out to be now not handiest a image of futuristic journey however also a cornerstone of complete, sustainable transportation worldwide.

CHAPTER 7

Technological Challenges of Hyperloop

7.1. Technology and Infrastructure Development

The improvement of Hyperloop technology affords a completely unique set of demanding situations, not handiest within the realm of advanced engineering but additionally inside the creation of the necessary infrastructure to support its modern transportation idea. At its middle, Hyperloop aims to deliver faster, greater green, and sustainable travel through using vacuum tubes and electromagnetic propulsion. However, to make this vision a fact, significant advancements need to be made in each era and infrastructure.

A key issue of Hyperloop's achievement lies in its propulsion gadget. The concept is constructed round a new mode of transportation where pods journey via near-vacuum tubes at speeds of as much as 760 miles per hour. This requires an electromagnetic propulsion machine, which makes use of magnetic fields to propel the pods without any bodily contact. The challenge right here is to broaden green, value-powerful, and scalable electromagnetic propulsion technologies. The primary system under attention is the linear synchronous motor (LSM), which is being examined and subtle for the Hyperloop venture. The assignment is to growth its efficiency, lessen energy consumption, and make it possible for massive-scale use.

In addition to the propulsion system, the power needed to force Hyperloop ought to come from renewable sources to preserve its sustainability credentials. Solar panels positioned on the exterior of the vacuum tubes or included into the infrastructure should assist offset the energy intake, making sure that the system operates in a more eco-friendly manner. One giant mission here is the development of light-weight, high-capacity electricity garage solutions that may deliver the vital power all through the entire journey.

Another middle factor of Hyperloop generation is the vacuum tube gadget. The idea in the back of Hyperloop is to create a near-vacuum surroundings in the tubes to lessen air resistance, allowing the pods to journey at distinctly high speeds. This is a massive departure from traditional transportation strategies that depend on open-air environments. Building and retaining a vacuum tube machine is an engineering assignment because of the want for close to-best seals to prevent air from leaking into the tube.

The vacuum tubes have to also be robust enough to face up to external pressures, which include earthquakes or severe climate situations, while maintaining their structural integrity. This requires the development of revolutionary substances and creation techniques. Steel and strengthened carbon-fiber composites are frequently considered for the tubes, however new, lighter, and extra long lasting substances might also come to be the generation matures. Additionally, the tubes should be geared up with energetic systems that may maintain the vacuum and reveal pressure ranges constantly.

Safety is a number one challenge for any transportation gadget, and Hyperloop is not any exception. The layout and production of the infrastructure want to make certain that the gadget is resilient in the face of natural disasters, accidents, and other surprising events. One key project is ensuring that the tubes are both especially long lasting and able to managing excessive situations, inclusive of earthquakes, extreme temperatures, and capability influences from debris or accidents.

Furthermore, protection functions have to include the improvement of emergency protocols and evacuation systems in case of system failure or other unforeseen problems. The Hyperloop system need to be able to retain functioning in destructive situations, and it should consist of backup systems for power, air deliver, and pod control. Designing a fail-safe mechanism that ensures the protection of passengers with out compromising the rate and performance of the transportation system is a main obstacle for engineers and designers.

Another essential task is the purchase of land for Hyperloop construction. In order for the gadget to become operational, huge stretches of land should be cleared and distinct for the development of the vacuum tubes and stations. In densely populated areas, this may be a full-size mission due to current infrastructure and the want to minimize disruptions to neighborhood groups.

Land acquisition methods frequently involve complicated felony and regulatory hurdles, in particular while the infrastructure passes thru multiple jurisdictions or affects protected land areas. Additionally, building the necessary stations, terminals, and interchanges requires careful making plans to integrate with existing city areas and transportation networks, all at the same time as ensuring that the Hyperloop machine can seamlessly join cities.

In the development of Hyperloop infrastructure, one ought to additionally do not forget the environmental impact of massive-scale creation tasks. While Hyperloop gives capability environmental benefits through decreased emissions and reliance on renewable energy, the construction of the essential infrastructure may additionally nonetheless make contributions to ecological disruption. Careful making plans must be applied to minimize the effect on natural world, local ecosystems, and natural landscapes.

Additionally, the substances utilized in production need to be sustainable and environmentally friendly. As Hyperloop infrastructure is developed, engineers must are seeking for solutions that decrease waste and ensure that the carbon footprint of the construction system stays as little as viable.

Finally, growing the vital era and infrastructure for Hyperloop requires good sized funding and collaboration between the private and non-private sectors. Many tasks of this scale and ambition face financial challenges, particularly in terms of the preliminary capital funding required to build infrastructure, broaden technology, and behavior vital research. The non-public area is frequently the driving pressure in the back of technological innovation, however the public sector must play a function in supplying funding, regulatory support, and incentives for infrastructure development.

Additionally, collaboration between governmental companies, nearby governments, and international bodies could be important for Hyperloop's worldwide deployment. Infrastructure initiatives of this value require pass-border cooperation and adherence to international standards, mainly in relation to protection, environmental rules, and inter-us of a transportation.

The development of Hyperloop era and infrastructure is a multifaceted venture that includes breakthroughs in propulsion, creation, and protection structures. As we pass forward with this ambitious challenge, addressing these technological demanding situations would require collaboration amongst professionals from more than one disciplines, giant investment, and the testing and refinement of novel techniques to transportation infrastructure. The a hit implementation of Hyperloop may not only revolutionize journey however also set a new widespread for worldwide transportation systems, offering quicker, extra sustainable, and efficient solutions for destiny generations.

7.2. Engineering and Design Challenges

The development of Hyperloop as a excessive-velocity transportation system calls for overcoming a multitude of complex engineering and design demanding situations. From the advent of the vacuum tubes to the development of the pod propulsion machine, each aspect of the Hyperloop have to be meticulously designed to ensure protection, performance, and scalability. These challenges are not just technical however additionally contain balancing fee, sustainability, and regulatory constraints at the same time as preserving the original imaginative and prescient of a faster, purifier, and greater green transportation network.

At the coronary heart of Hyperloop's layout is the pod, which need to be capable of travelling at speeds drawing close 760 miles in keeping with hour. The design of those pods is critical, as they must be both light-weight and especially long lasting, able to withstand the forces associated with high-speed tour even as retaining structural integrity. The pods additionally need to be aerodynamically optimized to limit drag in the low-pressure environment of the vacuum tube.

The materials used for pod creation are a first-rate attention in overcoming engineering challenges. Traditional materials which includes steel can be too heavy, whilst lightweight composites may not offer the necessary energy. To clear up this, designers are experimenting with quite a few advanced materials, which include carbon-fiber composites and graphene, which offer a stability of energy, lightness, and sturdiness. The pod must also have an efficient device to control heat, because the high-pace movement generates significant friction, even in a vacuum environment. Innovations in passive and active cooling technologies are being explored to preserve operational safety.

The vacuum tube, a essential element of the Hyperloop gadget, need to be designed to create a near-vacuum surroundings for pods to journey thru at high speeds. Maintaining such an surroundings calls for enormously specialised engineering answers to prevent air from leaking into the tube. This challenge involves growing tube materials which might be sturdy enough to handle the outside strain of the surroundings whilst maintaining an airtight seal. The vacuum tubes additionally want to be engineered to be resilient in opposition to environmental situations together with earthquakes, extreme temperatures, and weather-associated pressure.

Additionally, the tubes need to be elevated or set up in a way that guarantees they stay straight and stage across vast distances. Elevation may be accomplished thru using pylons or tunnels, both of which gift their personal layout challenges.

The shape ought to permit for minimal deformation over lengthy distances, accounting for capability shifts in the floor or the results of temperature adjustments that might purpose the material to increase or agreement. Innovative answers like the use of bendy, self-correcting materials are being taken into consideration to solve this difficulty.

One of the most good sized engineering demanding situations in Hyperloop generation is the development of a dependable and green propulsion gadget. The gadget is predicated on electromagnetic propulsion—especially, a linear synchronous motor (LSM)—to transport the pods through the vacuum tube. This technique of propulsion makes use of magnetic fields to push the pods forward, fending off the need for conventional mechanical contact or gas-based engines, which might generate friction and drastically reduce performance.

The layout of the LSM device ought to reap a sensitive balance between power and performance. It need to be effective sufficient to boost up the pods to excessive speeds quickly, yet green enough to reduce strength consumption and hold consistent pace over lengthy distances. In addition to the propulsion gadget, Hyperloop must also cope with the difficulty of braking. The deceleration gadget needs to be as efficient and secure because the propulsion gadget, capable of slowing the pods hastily with out causing undue pressure on passengers or the pod itself.

Given the acute speeds and power demands required for Hyperloop to function, designing an green and sustainable power gadget is any other vital mission. The power demands of the machine are vast, and powering it thru traditional approach should negate a few of the environmental benefits that Hyperloop promises. To address this, designers are searching at the opportunity of the use of renewable electricity resources consisting of sun energy, wind energy, or even tidal electricity to generate the desired electricity.

One of the most tough factors of this strength requirement is ensuring that the machine can save sufficient energy to function effectively and reliably. Energy storage technology, consisting of superior batteries and flywheels, are being explored to store electricity generated from renewable assets and deliver it to the gadget whilst wished. The storage device ought to be lightweight, pretty green, and able to supplying non-stop energy throughout the entire adventure.

Engineering the protection functions of Hyperloop provides numerous demanding situations. High-speed travel in a vacuum environment calls for the device to be resilient inside the face of various emergencies, inclusive of electricity disasters, machine malfunctions, and herbal screw ups. The pods ought to be designed to guard passengers inside the event of a failure, whether which means incorporating emergency braking systems or developing pods which can survive an effect or rapid deceleration.

In addition, engineers should layout an emergency evacuation gadget in the event of a chief disruption. This could include structures for rapidly depressurizing the vacuum tubes, imparting a secure go out for passengers, and allowing emergency responders to get entry to the system fast and efficaciously. While the overall purpose is to make the Hyperloop as safe as possible, the modern nature of the system provides precise demanding situations in waiting for and mitigating every feasible state of affairs.

The infrastructure required to assist Hyperloop spans thousands of miles, requiring cautious attention of the land use and integration with current infrastructure. The extended or underground tubes need to be positioned in locations that minimize disruption to the surrounding surroundings, such as densely populated city areas and guarded herbal landscapes. A vital component of infrastructure design is the capacity to combine Hyperloop stations and terminals into current towns and concrete transportation structures. Stations need to be strategically positioned in places that permit for clean get admission to to passengers whilst making sure that the network can make bigger and interconnect with other forms of transportation.

Additionally, the construction of the vital infrastructure requires good sized making plans concerning land acquisition, environmental effect checks, and felony considerations. Hyperloop's infrastructure will need to navigate complicated regulatory environments, and big-scale creation tasks will require the coordination of multiple governmental and private entities.

Finally, certainly one of the largest engineering demanding situations lies in making Hyperloop era scalable and financially feasible. Developing and trying out prototypes is an expensive process, and scaling the technology for mass adoption includes sizeable funding in infrastructure and ongoing studies and development. Hyperloop engineers should layout systems that may be produced and deployed at a reasonable value, even as making sure that the fine and overall performance of the device aren't compromised.

In the longer term, engineers must layout Hyperloop generation with scalability in thoughts. The gadget should be adaptable to a number of geographical environments, from city towns to faraway rural regions, and it must be scalable enough to accommodate the developing call for for transportation without straining the system's capabilities or infrastructure.

The engineering and layout challenges of Hyperloop are vast and multifaceted, requiring improvements in substances science, propulsion technology, strength structures, and infrastructure development. As with any groundbreaking transportation device, the street to consciousness is fraught with boundaries, however overcoming those challenges is vital to remodeling the Hyperloop concept into a feasible and sustainable transportation gadget. Engineers and designers will retain to push the limits of era and creativity to deliver this bold imaginative and prescient to existence, in the end shaping the destiny of travel for generations to come back.

7.3. Financial and Legal Barriers

The a success implementation of the Hyperloop system, like every huge-scale infrastructure task, faces large financial and felony challenges. These demanding situations not only effect the improvement of the technology however also its significant adoption and lengthy-time period sustainability. Addressing those monetary and legal barriers is important to make certain the venture can flow ahead and sooner or later transform transportation networks worldwide.

One of the most sizeable economic obstacles to the belief of the Hyperloop is the sheer magnitude of preliminary investment required. Building the infrastructure for Hyperloop—comprising vacuum tubes, expanded or underground tracks, stations, and other supporting centers— requires loads of billions of dollars. This prematurely price can be prohibitive, and the improvement of this type of modern era needs great investment. The great economic sources wanted for studies, design, trying out, and construction of Hyperloop structures gift a primary hurdle for non-public and public traders alike.

Hyperloop builders, together with private groups like Virgin Hyperloop and Elon Musk's The Boring Company, are actively seeking investment from both public and personal sectors. Government investment performs a critical function, as the general public sector is often greater inclined to put money into high-danger, long-time period initiatives with vast societal blessings. However, securing government investment for brand spanking new technologies is a complicated procedure, requiring political support, price range allocation, and alignment with public coverage dreams.

Investors additionally require assurance that Hyperloop will provide a return on funding ultimately, which ends up in worries approximately the gadget's financial viability. Profitability is unsure, especially given the lengthy timeline to increase and deploy the generation and the capability for fee overruns. In addition, competing transportation systems like excessive-speed trains, conventional air travel, and self sustaining motors also pose economic dangers, as those options have hooked up infrastructure and customer bases.

To conquer those economic challenges, the Hyperloop development community have to discover a whole lot of funding models, inclusive of public-private partnerships, task capital, and worldwide collaborations. Additionally, governments and private businesses have to discover ways to lessen the overall price of infrastructure creation, together with by means of utilizing modular designs, reducing labor prices, or leveraging current transportation networks.

Even if initial investment is secured, the long-term financial sustainability of Hyperloop is a prime difficulty. Hyperloop, like every big-scale transportation device, ought to operate effectively and sustainably over many years, and making sure its persisted profitability requires cautious monetary planning.

Operating expenses, along with preservation, strength consumption, and staffing, need to be carefully managed to make sure the device stays feasible. In addition, ticket expenses ought to be competitive with other modes of transportation, but sufficient to cover the operational and preservation prices. If the value of operating Hyperloop is too high, it can be relegated to a gap marketplace or conflict to advantage mass adoption.

Moreover, the effect of Hyperloop on current transportation infrastructure and industries need to be taken into consideration. For instance, traditional rail and airline industries might also withstand or be negatively laid low with the introduction of such a disruptive era. This should lead to criminal disputes and monetary tensions, in particular in areas in which installed industries are politically effective.

Beyond economic barriers, the felony and regulatory panorama presents sizable challenges to Hyperloop's improvement. Given that the device entails excessive-velocity journey in a vacuum environment, it have to follow more than a few protection, environmental, and operational policies. Each u.s. Or area in which Hyperloop is delivered can have its very own legal framework, creating a complex web of compliance necessities.

One of the primary worries from a felony attitude is passenger safety. Given the excessive speeds at which Hyperloop pods could travel, injuries or malfunctions, at the same time as not likely, could result in catastrophic consequences. Legal frameworks must be established to make sure that Hyperloop is held to the best protection standards, which includes enormous trying out, certification, and ongoing inspections.

Liability legal guidelines also want to be tailored to account for the specific risks associated with Hyperloop. In the event of an coincidence, determining responsibility for the purpose—whether it's far the layout, production, operation, or maintenance of the gadget—will probable require new felony precedents and changes to current liability laws. Hyperloop groups will want to put money into liability coverage and collaborate with governments to create a felony framework that protects both operators and passengers.

Hyperloop structures may also be problem to a whole lot of environmental rules, in particular in regards to land use. The construction of massive vacuum tubes and extended tracks would require the acquisition of large tracts of land, which may be in densely populated or environmentally sensitive areas. Developers will need to navigate complex zoning laws, environmental impact assessments, and nearby regulations to stable the essential land for the device.

Additionally, the environmental impact of the Hyperloop itself have to be assessed. While Hyperloop is touted as an environmentally pleasant alternative to conventional transportation, concerns approximately the effect of the gadget on wildlife, air quality, and noise pollution will want to be addressed. Regulatory our bodies would require thorough environmental impact exams to make certain the undertaking does not motive irreversible damage to ecosystems or groups.

Securing government acclaim for Hyperloop tasks is a complicated and time-consuming method. Governments need to be convinced of the lengthy-term advantages of the gadget, now not only in phrases of transportation but additionally in areas along with economic development, task creation, and environmental sustainability. This calls for alignment with national infrastructure desires, delivery policies, and monetary targets.

Moreover, because Hyperloop goals to connect towns throughout substantial distances, worldwide collaboration can be essential. Legal agreements need to be negotiated among international locations concerning land use, protection standards, customs techniques, and infrastructure integration. Political demanding situations may want to get up, especially when coping with differing regulatory regimes or competing transportation priorities.

The monetary and felony obstacles to Hyperloop's development are significant but now not insurmountable. Overcoming those challenges would require innovative solutions, robust political help, and collaboration among the public and private sectors. Financial backing must be secured to cover the initial investment and ongoing operational prices, while criminal frameworks need to evolve to address the particular risks and challenges posed by means of this new transportation system. As the Hyperloop keeps to transport from idea to reality, addressing those financial and legal troubles can be crucial to making sure the successful deployment of the era and its lengthy-time period sustainability.

7.4. Safety and Emergency Protocols

Ensuring protection within the Hyperloop device is paramount, given the unprecedented speeds and novel technology worried on this modern mode of transportation. Safety and emergency protocols are meticulously designed to address each habitual operational risks and surprising vital conditions, aiming to shield passengers, crew, and infrastructure while keeping public confidence within the era.

Hyperloop drugs perform inside near-vacuum tubes, remoted from external environmental factors such as weather, debris, or wildlife. This controlled environment inherently reduces many conventional risks faced by means of other transportation modes. However, the acute speeds and confined nature of the tubes introduce specific challenges that call for state-of-the-art protection structures. For instance, keeping structural integrity of the vacuum tubes is important; advanced substances with high durability and real-time structural health tracking ensure early detection of any capacity weaknesses or breaches.

A cornerstone of Hyperloop safety lies in its complete sensor community and automated manipulate structures. Constant monitoring of tube pressure, capsule role, pace, and environmental parameters allows instant detection of anomalies. In the occasion of irregularities, automated protocols can provoke managed deceleration, reroute drugs, or safely carry them to a halt. These systems minimize human errors and enable rapid, unique responses beyond human functionality, growing normal protection margins.

Emergency protocols are advanced to cowl a huge spectrum of situations, from minor technical faults to greater excessive incidents like tube depressurization or tablet malfunctions. Redundant protection layers are carried out to make sure gadget resilience, which include multiple braking structures, backup strength components, and fail-secure valves which could isolate tube sections in case of pressure loss. Passengers are blanketed via bolstered pill systems able to withstanding stress variations and equipped with lifestyles-assist systems to maintain breathable air and comfortable situations in the course of emergencies.

Evacuation strategies were a critical layout attention. Unlike traditional trains or airplanes in which passengers can evacuate at once onto tracks or runways, Hyperloop tablets function internal sealed tubes, posing challenges for speedy exit. To address this, emergency egress factors are included at everyday intervals along the tubes, prepared with stable get entry to tunnels and safety chambers. Capsules are designed to dock at those emergency stations, where passengers may be effectively transferred and evacuated. Additionally, rescue motors capable of navigating inside the tubes can be deployed if vital.

Staff schooling and passenger conversation are essential to safety protocols. Operators undergo rigorous education to handle regular operations and emergencies, supported by simulation-based totally drills. Passengers receive clean instructions and get right of entry to to emergency facts through onboard structures, ensuring calm and coordinated responses throughout incidents.

Regulatory standards for Hyperloop safety are evolving in tandem with technological development. Collaboration among governments, international agencies, and enterprise stakeholders goals to establish complete frameworks that set rigorous benchmarks for layout, trying out, and operation. These requirements not most effective defend customers but additionally facilitate public believe and regulatory approval crucial for great adoption.

The protection and emergency protocols of Hyperloop are built on superior generation, redundancy, and meticulous making plans to manage the specific risks of extremely-excessive-pace vacuum transit. From real-time tracking to strong structural designs and emergency evacuation techniques, every component is engineered to prioritize passenger nicely-being and gadget resilience. As Hyperloop movements closer to operational reality, its safety systems will maintain to conform, placing new paradigms for stable and reliable transportation inside the cutting-edge era.

CHAPTER 8

The Future of Hyperloop: Potential and Investment

8.1. Future Applications of Hyperloop

As a cutting-edge transportation era, Hyperloop has the ability to revolutionize no longer most effective passenger travel but also freight transportation, urban planning, and worldwide alternate. Its excessive-velocity, low-strength, and environmentally friendly design opens up new avenues for packages that would reshape industries, economies, and day by day life across the globe. The Hyperloop concept is going past simply replacing conventional trains or motors; it's miles poised to modify the entire landscape of transportation infrastructure and interconnectivity. Here, we are able to discover the destiny packages of Hyperloop, highlighting its potential to transform various sectors and address the developing demands for extra efficient, sustainable, and fee-effective transportation systems.

The number one and most widely predicted utility of Hyperloop is in the realm of high-speed intercity journey. By connecting predominant cities with close to-supersonic speeds—potentially exceeding 700 miles consistent with hour (1,100 kilometers in keeping with hour)—Hyperloop should drastically lessen travel times between metropolitan regions which are presently numerous hours apart by means of vehicle or conventional train.

For example, Hyperloop should link towns like Los Angeles and San Francisco in just half-hour, compared to a 6-

hour power or a 2-hour flight. This should substantially beautify enterprise interactions, tourism, and each day commuting across regions which can be presently separated by long journey times. The potential to make lengthy-distance journey extra handy, low-priced, and efficient might also encourage the decentralization of populations, lowering overcrowding in fundamental urban facilities even as facilitating financial boom in smaller cities and areas.

Beyond lengthy-haul intercity tour, Hyperloop should play a transformative position in enhancing suburban and regional connectivity. For towns facing congestion and confined area for enlargement, Hyperloop systems should provide a solution for alleviating city sprawl and offering commuters a quick, efficient way to travel between suburban areas and town facilities. The capability to construct underground or expanded routes might permit for the mixing of Hyperloop inside current urban landscapes with out disrupting surface-stage infrastructure.

In regions where present day public transportation systems are insufficient, Hyperloop may want to offer a speedy, excessive-ability alternative to buses and trains, decreasing tour times and offering a extra reliable mode of transportation. With decrease running prices than conventional systems, it may offer a feasible alternative to the an increasing number of congested highways and railways in lots of elements of the world.

While a whole lot of the point of interest has been on passenger travel, Hyperloop technology holds incredible promise for the freight and logistics industries. By leveraging the equal high-pace, low-resistance vacuum tube system, Hyperloop may be used to move items efficaciously throughout large distances. Cargo Hyperloop pods may want to tour at speeds similar to cutting-edge air freight offerings however at a far decrease price, imparting an unprecedented aggregate of velocity, performance, and affordability.

This fast and secure mode of transporting goods should reduce transport times from days to mere hours, probably reworking worldwide supply chains. Hyperloop may be in particular beneficial for time-touchy deliveries, consisting of perishable items, prescription drugs, and high-price products. It might additionally reduce the environmental footprint of freight shipping, providing a greater sustainable solution in comparison to traditional transport strategies like trucks and airplanes, which can be greater reliant on fossil fuels.

As urban areas continue to grow and evolve, Hyperloop can be an necessary a part of smart metropolis projects. Smart cities utilize interconnected technologies and statistics-driven systems to optimize the flow of people, goods, and information. Hyperloop's velocity and efficiency align nicely with the goals of smart metropolis designs, as it could offer a rapid, sustainable method to urban mobility demanding situations.

Hyperloop stations might be incorporated with present transportation infrastructure which include buses, subways, and mild rail structures, creating seamless multi-modal networks for urban commuters. In addition, the actual-time records abilties of clever towns could enhance the Hyperloop experience, imparting passengers with updated information on tour times, gadget fame, and ability delays. Hyperloop should end up a principal issue of city mobility structures, imparting a high-velocity alternative to different forms of public transportation while lowering site visitors congestion and improving air first-class.

Hyperloop's potential extends past national borders, as its excessive-pace, low-value layout ought to facilitate worldwide travel and connectivity in methods that have by no means been viable earlier than. The capacity to travel between nations in only a few hours would have a profound impact on worldwide change, tourism, and cultural alternate. For example, Hyperloop ought to provide a greater low-cost and environmentally pleasant alternative to lengthy-haul flights, specifically for countries with strong monetary ties and geographical proximity.

An international Hyperloop network may want to join main hubs throughout continents, allowing fast travel between towns like New York, London, and Dubai. As the generation matures and the systems are integrated throughout international locations, it could create a brand new era of worldwide connectivity, enhancing monetary collaboration, fostering worldwide exchange, and making it less complicated for humans to experience different cultures and regions.

Hyperloop's environmental blessings increase beyond decreasing emissions in passenger transport. As a smooth strength solution, Hyperloop may want to play an essential role inside the global push in the direction of sustainability. With its minimum reliance on fossil fuels and its capability for being powered by means of renewable electricity sources including sun and wind, Hyperloop may want to assist reduce the transportation region's normal carbon footprint, which is considered one of the largest members to weather change.

Furthermore, Hyperloop ought to combine with other sustainable transportation technology, consisting of electric powered vehicles and renewable strength grids, growing a holistic, low-carbon delivery atmosphere. The environmentally friendly nature of Hyperloop may want to entice authorities guide and public funding, in particular as governments round the sector ramp up their efforts to fight weather trade.

Tourism could be transformed by using the creation of Hyperloop, as vacationers should easily get entry to some distance-flung locations in a fragment of the time it currently takes. For instance, tourists in Europe may want to easily journey between fundamental towns like Paris, Rome, and Barcelona, all within an hour or two. This would allow for weekend trips to multiple destinations, allowing tourism to flourish in areas previously hard to get right of entry to within a single ride.

Additionally, Hyperloop should open up new avenues for amusement travel to extra remote or lesser-regarded destinations, assisting to promote sustainable tourism in regions which can be regularly bypassed via traditional transport networks. This should stimulate financial growth in less-evolved areas and allow for the equitable distribution of tourism benefits throughout wider regions.

Hyperloop can also subsequently play a role in facilitating get right of entry to to spaceports for suborbital and interplanetary journey. As organizations like SpaceX and Blue Origin enhance the improvement of space tourism and space exploration technology, the need for rapid, efficient shipping to spaceports becomes more and more essential. Hyperloop should offer a fast and fee-effective approach of having passengers to spaceports for his or her journeys, enhancing the efficiency of area travel operations.

The integration of Hyperloop with spaceports could also lessen the want for conventional airport infrastructure, allowing a extra streamlined, futuristic approach to area tourism. This may want to make space tour extra on hand and affordable, finally developing a new mode of transportation beyond Earth's environment.

Hyperloop's potential programs make bigger some distance past its initial imaginative and prescient of excessive-speed intercity tour. Its capacity to decorate international connectivity, streamline freight transportation, contribute to environmental sustainability, and combine with rising technologies like area travel and clever cities makes it one of the most promising improvements of the 21st century. As the generation keeps to conform, the destiny of Hyperloop should reshape whole industries, create new economic opportunities, and remodel the manner we flow across the globe. Its great implementation may want to cause a transportation revolution, providing quicker, extra sustainable, and value-powerful solutions for both people and goods, even as additionally enhancing the interconnectedness of our worldwide society.

8.2. Investors and Global Collaborations

The realization of Hyperloop technology is not solely dependent on innovation and engineering advancements but also on securing robust investments and fostering strategic global collaborations. Given the scale of investment required for infrastructure development, as well as the potential market opportunities, Hyperloop's future is intertwined with the support of private investors, government initiatives, and international partnerships.

Private investment plays a pivotal role in advancing any emerging technology, especially one as ambitious as Hyperloop. As a long-term project with high upfront costs and uncertain timelines, securing funding from investors is essential for conducting research, development, and testing phases. The private sector, including venture capital firms, angel investors, and large corporations, has shown increasing interest in the Hyperloop concept due to its disruptive potential and ability to redefine transportation.

Several prominent companies have already committed substantial investments to the development of Hyperloop technology. For example, Virgin Hyperloop, backed by Richard Branson's Virgin Group, has been actively involved in developing prototypes, conducting tests, and pursuing regulatory approval in various countries. In addition to Virgin Hyperloop, Elon Musk's The Boring Company, and other startups have made significant strides in perfecting the technology. Such investment is not only financial but also strategic, with investors seeking to capitalize on the emerging transportation sector, expected to be worth billions in the coming decades.

Furthermore, investments in Hyperloop are seen as opportunities to diversify portfolios in the growing fields of clean energy, sustainable infrastructure, and high-tech mobility solutions. As climate change and environmental concerns take center stage in global policy debates, companies that prioritize sustainability and low-emission technologies are likely to attract investments, particularly from firms and individuals looking to support green innovation.

While private investments are crucial, government involvement is equally important for large-scale infrastructure projects such as Hyperloop. Governments can provide funding, regulatory support, and access to public infrastructure, all of which are necessary to facilitate the widespread implementation of Hyperloop systems. The cost of constructing the necessary tubes, stations, and other infrastructure is astronomical, making public funding a critical enabler.

Public-private partnerships (PPPs) have already been proposed as a potential model to fund and develop Hyperloop systems. By working together, governments and private companies can share both the financial burden and the rewards. Governments can provide access to land, regulatory approval, and public transportation data, while private investors bring in the technical expertise and financial capital needed to develop the systems. These collaborations can help minimize the risks associated with large-scale infrastructure projects and provide the necessary support for Hyperloop's widespread rollout.

Several governments around the world have expressed interest in working with Hyperloop companies to bring this technology to their regions. For instance, India, the United Arab Emirates (UAE), and the United States have all shown enthusiasm for exploring Hyperloop systems as part of their transportation infrastructure plans. In many cases, governments are offering incentives, such as subsidies, grants, and tax breaks, to encourage investment in the development and implementation of Hyperloop technology.

Hyperloop technology is a highly interdisciplinary field that requires expertise across various domains, including engineering, physics, material science, and transportation planning. To fully realize the potential of Hyperloop, global collaborations in research and development (R&D) are essential. These partnerships can help share knowledge, pool resources, and accelerate progress in overcoming the technological challenges associated with building a fully functional Hyperloop system.

Collaborations between universities, research institutions, and private companies will play a critical role in improving the technology and making it commercially viable. For example, academic institutions may contribute research on advanced propulsion systems, energy storage solutions, and materials that can withstand the extreme conditions inside Hyperloop tubes. Private companies, on the other hand, can bring in practical knowledge and real-world expertise in system design, manufacturing, and testing.

International collaboration will also be important for addressing the complex logistical and regulatory challenges involved in implementing Hyperloop systems across borders. To ensure that Hyperloop operates efficiently and safely in different countries, stakeholders must coordinate on issues such as safety standards, environmental regulations, and land-use policies. Global cooperation will also be necessary to design and build cross-border Hyperloop networks, especially for systems that link multiple countries or continents.

Beyond government and academic collaborations, strategic partnerships with key players in other industries will be instrumental in driving Hyperloop's development. One of the primary industries that will benefit from collaborating with Hyperloop companies is the construction and engineering sector. Building the infrastructure required for Hyperloop systems will involve massive construction efforts, including the development of underground tunnels, stations, and support facilities. Strategic partnerships with construction firms will help reduce costs, improve construction efficiency, and ensure the highest levels of safety during the building process.

In addition, partnerships with energy companies will be essential, as Hyperloop systems will require a substantial amount of electricity to operate. As sustainability is a key focus of Hyperloop's design, collaborating with renewable energy providers will be crucial in powering the system in an environmentally friendly way. By integrating solar, wind, and other renewable energy sources, Hyperloop systems can become self-sustaining and further reduce their carbon footprint.

Hyperloop companies may also need to form alliances with tech companies specializing in artificial intelligence, machine learning, and automation. These technologies will be essential for ensuring the efficient operation of Hyperloop systems, from managing passenger flow and scheduling to optimizing energy usage and monitoring system performance in real-time. Collaboration with companies specializing in cybersecurity will also be necessary to protect the system from cyber threats, ensuring safe and secure travel for all passengers.

As Hyperloop moves from prototype to reality, its ability to expand on a global scale will depend on the involvement of multinational corporations (MNCs) that can facilitate its growth in different regions. These corporations bring with them the global networks, capital, and infrastructure needed to scale Hyperloop technology beyond a few select markets.

For instance, large-scale engineering firms, global banks, and technology giants can help with financing, building, and deploying Hyperloop systems worldwide. By partnering with these companies, Hyperloop firms can leverage existing infrastructure, supply chains, and market knowledge to accelerate the system's deployment across regions with high transportation demand. MNCs with a presence in multiple countries will also be instrumental in navigating the complex regulatory and business landscapes in different parts of the world.

Through international expansion, Hyperloop can become a global solution to transportation challenges, allowing people and goods to move faster and more efficiently across borders. As more countries and regions invest in the technology, the network of Hyperloop systems will grow, creating a truly interconnected world.

The development and implementation of Hyperloop technology will depend on a diverse array of investments and global collaborations. Private investors, governments, research institutions, and multinational corporations all play critical roles in ensuring the success of this revolutionary transportation system. By pooling resources, knowledge, and expertise, stakeholders can overcome the technological, financial, and regulatory challenges that stand in the way of Hyperloop's widespread adoption. Ultimately, the strength of these global collaborations will determine whether Hyperloop can achieve its full potential and become a transformative force in the future of transportation.

8.3. The Role of Hyperloop in the Global Economy

As a revolutionary transportation system, Hyperloop has the potential to profoundly influence the global economy. By dramatically reducing travel time, cutting costs, and improving efficiency, Hyperloop can transform not only the transportation sector but also industries ranging from logistics and manufacturing to tourism and real estate.

The introduction of Hyperloop technology will open new market opportunities across various sectors. One of the most significant effects of Hyperloop will be its ability to foster economic growth by improving connectivity between regions, thereby facilitating more efficient movement of people and goods. Hyperloop's potential to reduce transportation time between major cities and industrial hubs could increase productivity and open up previously untapped markets.

By linking geographically distant areas more effectively, Hyperloop could promote the emergence of new economic clusters. These interconnected economic regions would benefit from shared resources, labor, and expertise, creating a more integrated global economy. The speed at which goods and services can be delivered will revolutionize global supply chains, creating a more dynamic and flexible market. Faster transit times will result in quicker delivery of products, reduced inventory costs, and increased efficiency, especially in sectors like manufacturing, retail, and agriculture.

Additionally, the construction and operation of Hyperloop systems would generate significant economic activity. The infrastructure projects required to build the tubes, stations, and supporting systems would provide employment opportunities and stimulate investment in local economies. Once operational, the Hyperloop system would drive economic growth by improving access to labor markets, enabling companies to tap into broader talent pools.

Hyperloop's ability to drastically shorten travel times between cities and countries could have a transformative impact on international trade. By connecting major trade hubs in a matter of hours instead of days, it will become possible to ship goods with greater speed and efficiency, making cross-border commerce more seamless. This will allow businesses to reduce costs, streamline logistics, and open up new opportunities for global expansion.

The high-speed movement of goods and services will also create new opportunities for international collaboration. With faster transit times, countries and regions that were previously economically isolated due to distance or transportation inefficiencies will be able to integrate into the global supply chain. Hyperloop could reduce transportation costs, which, in turn, will lead to cheaper products for consumers and improved profitability for businesses engaged in international trade.

Hyperloop could also play a critical role in the development of global e-commerce. By enabling fast, reliable delivery of goods across vast distances, it could improve the efficiency of the global logistics network, offering consumers quicker access to a broader range of products. The resulting demand for high-speed transportation infrastructure would benefit not only manufacturers and retailers but also logistics companies that specialize in the movement of goods across countries and continents.

Hyperloop could significantly reshape the tourism industry by making travel more accessible and affordable. Its high-speed connections between major cities would enable tourists to travel quickly and conveniently, opening up new possibilities for vacation destinations. The ability to easily reach distant regions would encourage more people to explore different countries and cultures, boosting international tourism and increasing spending in the hospitality, entertainment, and travel industries.

For business travelers, Hyperloop would make it possible to attend meetings, conferences, and events across regions without the time constraints typically associated with long-distance air travel. In particular, executives and professionals could save valuable time by traveling quickly between cities for short trips, increasing productivity and improving the efficiency of business operations. This increased mobility could further stimulate economic activity, especially in sectors such as conferences, trade fairs, and professional services.

Hyperloop's influence on mobility will extend beyond leisure and business travel. As more people and goods move at greater speeds, the system will help promote the exchange of ideas, innovation, and knowledge on a global scale. Hyperloop would act as a catalyst for cultural, economic, and technological exchanges, accelerating the global flow of information and ideas that are essential for continued progress in the 21st century.

The introduction of Hyperloop technology will create new job opportunities across multiple industries, ranging from transportation and construction to engineering and technology. The construction of Hyperloop infrastructure would generate thousands of jobs in the short term, as skilled labor will be required for tunnel digging, station building, and system installation. These jobs would not only provide economic benefits to the regions where Hyperloop systems are being built but also stimulate the growth of supporting industries, such as materials suppliers, manufacturing, and technology services.

Once operational, Hyperloop systems would require a variety of roles, including engineers, maintenance personnel, security staff, and customer service representatives. Additionally, the widespread use of Hyperloop could lead to an increase in demand for professionals in the fields of artificial intelligence, data analysis, cybersecurity, and transportation management, as these technologies will be critical to the efficient functioning of Hyperloop systems.

One of the key aspects of Hyperloop's potential impact on the global economy is its ability to transform the workforce. As more people have access to high-speed transportation, geographical barriers to employment would be reduced. This would enable workers to commute longer distances or even relocate for work without the time and cost limitations associated with traditional transportation. In turn, this could result in a more flexible and mobile workforce, capable of contributing to a wide range of industries and economic activities.

Hyperloop's potential to revolutionize transportation will influence global competitiveness by giving early adopters a competitive edge in the global economy. Countries and companies that invest in Hyperloop technology and infrastructure early on will gain significant advantages, particularly in industries dependent on logistics, technology, and high-speed transportation. As a result, nations that lead in Hyperloop development could see an increase in foreign direct investment and improved economic positioning on the global stage.

Furthermore, the demand for advanced technologies and innovation in the development of Hyperloop systems will drive further progress in industries such as engineering, robotics, materials science, and renewable energy. As the transportation sector evolves, Hyperloop will act as a testing ground for new technologies that will have far-reaching applications in other sectors, ranging from smart cities to autonomous vehicles.

The technological and economic success of Hyperloop could also foster greater competition among countries to develop their own high-speed transportation systems, leading to a global race for innovation in infrastructure and transportation technologies. This competition could spur additional investments in research and development and encourage more efficient, cost-effective solutions to transportation challenges around the world.

The global economy stands to benefit greatly from the widespread adoption of Hyperloop technology. Its ability to enhance international trade, create jobs, and improve efficiency in a variety of sectors will have a profound impact on the world economy. Hyperloop has the potential to connect distant regions, promote global collaboration, and stimulate economic growth across industries, transforming the way we think about mobility, infrastructure, and global competitiveness. As nations and companies work together to develop and implement Hyperloop systems, its role in shaping the future of the global economy will continue to expand, creating new opportunities and challenges for the generations to come.

8.4. Regulatory Frameworks and Global Standards

As Hyperloop era advances from conceptual innovation toward business deployment, the established order of strong regulatory frameworks and worldwide standards turns into vital to ensure its safe, efficient, and equitable integration into the arena's transportation systems. The precise characteristics of Hyperloop—running in close to-vacuum environments, utilising electromagnetic propulsion, and achieving unparalleled speeds—pose regulatory challenges that cutting-edge transportation laws and recommendations do now not completely address. Developing coherent, across the world identified guidelines and requirements is important for fostering public accept as true with, facilitating cross-border operations, and selling sustainable growth of this transformative generation.

Regulatory frameworks for Hyperloop need to encompass a complete variety of factors which include protection certification, environmental impact, technical specs, and operational protocols. Given the novelty of the era, regulators face the dual assignment of enabling innovation at the same time as preventing ability dangers. This calls for collaborative efforts among governments, industry leaders, technical professionals, and global bodies to create flexible but rigorous requirements. These frameworks have to stability encouraging research and funding with shielding passenger welfare and environmental sustainability.

International cooperation is in particular essential. Hyperloop routes are probably to span more than one jurisdictions, necessitating harmonized policies that allow seamless operations throughout borders. Without such alignment, variations in safety necessities, production codes, or operational licenses should create obstacles, increase charges, and put off assignment implementation. Establishing global standards additionally helps technology sharing and joint ventures, accelerating development and deployment international.

Key areas addressed by way of regulatory our bodies consist of structural integrity of vacuum tubes, electromagnetic emission controls, emergency reaction tactics, statistics protection, and passenger rights. Standards for creation materials, protection schedules, and system redundancy make sure long-term reliability and safety. In parallel, environmental regulations cognizance on minimizing the carbon footprint, maintaining herbal habitats for the duration of infrastructure improvement, and selling sustainable cloth usage.

Regulatory oversight extends beyond bodily infrastructure to include virtual and operational domain names. Cybersecurity protocols are important to protect the automated manipulate systems that manipulate Hyperloop pods and tube environments. Transparent facts reporting and monitoring make certain compliance and allow continuous development. Additionally, accessibility requirements assure that Hyperloop systems serve diverse populations, consisting of human beings with disabilities.

The improvement of those frameworks is supported by way of pilot tasks and trying out centers, which provide valuable information to inform coverage decisions. Governments and regulatory businesses often collaborate with Hyperloop developers at some stage in those phases, allowing real-world evaluation of protection measures, operational performance, and environmental influences. Lessons found out from those trials manual the refinement of requirements before complete-scale industrial deployment.

Economic concerns additionally affect regulatory layout. Policymakers should address problems which includes fare law, competition with current transportation providers, and incentives for sustainable practices. Clear regulatory pathways reduce investment uncertainty and inspire non-public-sector participation. At the equal time, oversight mechanisms guard public hobbies via preventing monopolistic behaviors and ensuring equitable access.

Establishing regulatory frameworks and international standards for Hyperloop technology is a complicated however critical undertaking. It requires worldwide collaboration, adaptive guidelines, and a holistic method that covers technical, environmental, operational, and social dimensions. Through thoughtful regulation, Hyperloop can effectively and sustainably realise its ability to revolutionize transportation on a worldwide scale, fostering innovation even as safeguarding the well-being of passengers and groups alike.